The Grid:

Lessons from the Men of Grindr

Part 2

LEX, ESQ.

ISBN-13: 978-1705308707

DEDICATION

To Jazzmyn, Elisabeth, Cassandra, Alisa and Dr. Jeff, for lending your time to make these stories shine and decrease the likelihood that any readers come for me in the reviews.

CONTENTS

ACKNOWLEDGMENTS

Right toward the end of undergrad, I was dealing with major depression. During that period, I documented my thoughts in a journal on my MacBook. I recently read the entirety of that journal. Many of the posts disturbed me, and it became clear how low I actually was. I once wrote, "life is ultimately the same cycle of feelings and emotions experienced in different contexts. Once you feel every core emotion, there is nothing left for you to miss out on."

In a later post, I wrote about a revelation. After years of ups and downs, it clicked to me that depression was truly a smart person's disease. Depression gives you an unhealthy and hyper-awareness of the harsh realities of life. I was sulking in these realities, and they were consuming me. I realized that my only way out was to use my thoughts – this hyper-awareness of the world around me – to try to affect some change. That would be my mission to distract me from a thought process that was spiraling me out of sanity.

Brewing concurrently were my own realizations about my sexuality. I experienced my first love, and I experienced my first heartbreak. I was introduced to the world of Grindr. I experienced new friends, new romances, and everything in between. I experienced joy, pain, and heartbreak with unprecedented impact and frequency. After years of experiences and frustration, I decided to make my page @theproblemgays. At that time, I made absolutely no connection to this being the "mission" I had hypothesized about years ago in my journal. I was just frustrated and needed to vent.

Only now do I realize that @theproblemgays is the embodiment of what I had predicted long ago. I took this hyper-awareness of issues in my community, and spun it into something that could help others. Help others vent, laugh, and reflect. Over the years, you all have sent me thousands of messages, e-mails, and comments to tell me that something I wrote was relatable to you or helped you with a tough situation you were going through. I once wrote in that same journal, "If something I create can help *one person* think or have a newfound awareness, then what I have created was worthwhile." You all have helped me accomplish that mission many times over.

With my page, it seems like *I'm* the one helping others — but anyone who has supported me has no idea how much they actually help *me*. You all have given me a purpose beyond myself, and it has helped keep me sane. To anyone going through a dark time reading this, please know that you are not alone, and do not give up on yourself. What is within you right now may feel like a sickness, but it is truly a power and a gift. With the proper treatment and support, you can turn even the lowest point in your life into something positive.

After publishing part one of this book I was often asked, "Are you nervous about how people will react?" The answer is no. I am sharing my experiences in what I feel is a fair light to the men involved in them. So much time has passed since these relationships that I would hope I could sit down with most of these guys, laugh about these stories, and mutually agree that our experiences will help others. Of course it's strange to have the equivalent of my diary available for all in print, but hearing feedback on how relatable part one has been solidifies that this process is worthwhile.
Not much has changed when it comes to online relationships in the past year. Grindr and similar apps continue to have a major impact on how our community connects and finds love. I think part one of *The Grid* was a solid start to exploring how Grindr impacts our community. Unfortunately, as soon as it was published, I thought of so many more things I wanted to say on the topic. I hope that this second and (spoiler alert — final) part of this book does justice to the labyrinth of dick and dysfunction this app has brought to the forefront of the gay community.

[1] INTRODUCTION: THE FIRST NIGHT

I never really wanted to share this story. It always felt too personal and too much like a failure. That said, I recognize that the memories we least desire to share can have the greatest potential impact. This is a story that predates Grindr, but has so much to do with my relationship to the app scene in general. I often reflect on this as the inciting incident that triggered years of online love, lust, and disappointment.

He was following me in an older black Jeep Grand Cherokee in pursuit of what, unbeknownst to him, would be my first "intimate gay experience." In retrospect, this moment should have been much more special, or at least have happened with someone I knew for more than 5 minutes. I met him earlier that evening via a Craigslist M4M posting.

But first, some backstory. Before apps, geolocation, and damn near 5G browsing in the palm of your hand, there was the Internet via PC's (personal computers, for the youth). I am not qualified to speak on some of the first websites geared toward gay interaction (I'm thinking Adam4Adam which, ironically, is also now an app); however, one of my earliest conduits to exploring sexuality was Craigslist. The M4M (read: men seeking men) page on Craigslist had a slew of extremely creepy ads for the many things strange men wanted to do with people they had never met online. No, I was not desperate enough to meet with one of these men. But between every ten or so of these "hell no" ads were generally brief but enticing postings from young men within your metro area who were equally as confused and curious as you about their sexuality.

The ads that most attracted me were rather innocent. Someone like a college student (ideally at the same school as me or one nearby) who was bi curious and looking for a friend with benefits to "explore" with. In a time when I was fully closeted, these Craigslist ads were my first glimpse into the concept that it wasn't only me that didn't feel super gay but also wouldn't mind exploring the idea that I was, extremely discreetly. Speaking of discreet, these ads notoriously misspelled the version of discreet meaning private as *discrete* – which means separate or distinct. It warms my heart to draw attention to that issue in permanent print. The younger snob in me would so quickly judge the ads that spelled discreet incorrectly, deeming those men unworthy of this inevitably awkward first gay hookup I was seeking. After years of solitude, my inner-snob is more than accepting of typos so long as a man is regularly talking to me (a feat in and of itself).

At any rate, I regularly browsed these pages after a long day at school, when I finally had time to focus on what was honestly my lowest priority – the fact that I might be gay. I will also admit that I often posted similar ads for myself, finding it easier for guys to e-mail me directly so I could weed out the crazies. If seeking a gay hookup were Teen Vogue, I was Lisa Love and you were Lauren and Whitney applying for an internship in matchy-matchy outfits. In short, I was judgmental, but mostly I wanted to highlight early on that this second book will not save you from my *The Hills* references. At any rate, receiving e-mails from others brought this secret yet exciting pursuit to my attention throughout the day. And yes, I had a secret Yahoo e-mail account for such purposes (talk about doing mid 2000's closeted right). One way or another, I began the interaction in question with

– let's call him Jason – late on a weekend evening.

You know that feeling when you are talking to someone you are interested in but something about the connection just isn't right? For instance, you ask them three questions and they only answer one, or they have really short answers, and overall, just don't have the same communication style as you? I think I just heard a collective "yes bitch" from readers. Well, that was Jason. The single – yes *single* – blurry photo he sent me was somewhat enticing, but his answers to my questions weren't doing much for his cause. I knew he had muscles and was maybe in the military, which was foreign and exciting for me at the time, but that's pretty much it. He wasn't open to answering too many questions, and that was counter to my process of feeling comfortable to meet someone randomly from the Internet. Kids – I've said it before and I'll say it again – if anything doesn't feel right about the person you're meeting, do not succumb to your hormones and do it anyway. Also, meet people in public places at first and if they refuse, just don't meet them. I promise you, the potential few moments of pleasure are not worth risking your life.

Anyway, at this point in time and contrary to the wealth of stranger danger fear I have now acquired, I agreed to meet Jason in a non-public place. Our interactions had left me in a "take it or leave it" position. Basically, if I wanted to meet and "explore" with the blurry muscular guy in the photo, he only had a couple hours of time – right now – and wasn't willing to alter his terms. To his credit, he wasn't completely horrible and did try to comfort me with slightly more thorough responses to some of my questions. I have to believe he wasn't completely terrifying for me to continue the conversation.

Thinking back, I must have been exceptionally desperate at this time. Many of these Craigslist M4M interactions had not panned out. I think a lot of guys similar to me were ultimately too afraid to meet. There were several guys at my school or who worked near me that I would message and even text for weeks to no avail. The texters were pretty serious – I actually cannot believe the number of guys who wouldn't give out their phone number in that era out of fear that they would get outed. Like I was going to subpoena their identity from Verizon and post a gay exposé on Facebook. Anyway, after many of these guys that felt *more right* flaked on me, I was really eager to get whatever this "first experience" was going to be over with so I could figure out if this whole gay thing was for me.

Back to that evening – here he was, following me in his Grand Cherokee. I knew that all of the circumstances surrounding this were textbook wrong, but I felt like I had come too far to drop this now. I had met him 10 minutes earlier, at a deserted shopping center off of a freeway exit. I guess you could call this our "first date," and we were driving to what would be our "second date" 20 minutes later. It felt less cheap that way, like hey – I already know this guy. When I met him, he was not like I imagined from his photo. Of course, the photo was purposefully blurry, so I don't know what I was imagining. I guess the blur gave me room to attribute some of my ideal features on his face.

Well, he wasn't my dream guy, but at least the muscles were honest. We had nothing in common, and that initial 10-minute parking lot meeting was definitely not enough to make me comfortable about any of this. I supposed mentally I had already decided that he was "good enough" for this first experience – and the then-econ major in me did not feel that the opportunity cost of skipping this experience was worth many more months of being flaked on. For context, I later switched my major because the math was too hard, so my economic-model-based decision-making was likely off. Nonetheless, we continued driving in caravan fashion to a different part of town, which was in the direction that he needed to go anyway to get "back to his base." I guess I believe that he was actually in the military, or some variant of it. I didn't ask, and he didn't tell. I guess we *did* have that unfortunate repression in common.

We arrived at a relatively deserted location. My heart was racing out of control, even before I got out of my car. I wasn't sure what this was going to be, but at this point I knew it had to be something.

I wasted too much of his time and I consciously skipped many potential opportunities to get away from him. Clearly, a part of me wanted this to happen – but why did it have to feel so wrong? The whole thing felt desperate and secretive – not knowing one another, meeting in sketchy parking lots behind the false security of window tint. It didn't help that he was a closet case older than me, giving me nothing to look up to. But when closeted, you only really feel comfortable doing these things with guys in your position who have just as much to hide, and just as much to lose.

I got in his car and we drove a block or so away, to an even more remote location, no doubt because I was freaking out over the remote possibility that we would get caught. In what was possibly my shortest and most awkward hookup experience, the whole ordeal was over more quickly that I had assumed. As most of my gay (and straight) readers will hopefully relate – that first experience is never anything quite like you expect. I think in the generation of idealized pornography as your only reference point for how it *should* be, most people are left feeling pretty disappointed. Not to say this several minute experience brought me even remotely close to a "home run" (in the baseball sex lexicon), but it was bad enough to make me feel absolutely horrible about myself. This wasn't the guy or situation that was going to make me feel good about potentially being gay – it was rushed, it was uncomfortable, it was scary. He was the worst of all worlds – more experienced than me, but still inexperienced and closeted enough to make the whole thing feel wrong and, honestly, like a wasted moment.

The worst part of this ordeal wasn't that night, however. The worst part came in the weeks, and months to follow. Unfortunately, this was not due to me, or Jason, or what took place on that night. Rather, the period of anguish that so many young gay people feel after this first experience is due to years of repressed feelings, severe guilt, and the complete lack of a support system to deal with the aftermath. Instantly, I felt dirty. I experienced a significant internal "falling from grace."

Whether wrong or right, up to this point in my life I had felt relatively perfect. I was a good student, a good son, a good friend, and a hard worker. And even though my romantic life really has no connection to those attributes, I guess this was my first time experiencing what I perceived as a major personal failure. I felt like I consciously made a really bad choice and I couldn't turn back. I remember interacting with my parents in the following days and not being able to look them in their eyes, as if direct eye contact would illuminate that I wasn't the person I was before. I had failed them, I had failed myself – I had succumbed to these evil feelings that had been brewing in me for years and acted upon them.

In writing that, it sounds like I was raised super religiously – but I wasn't. It doesn't take religion to internalize homophobia – society honestly does a great job by itself (although I hope that is changing with time). I continued feeling broken and empty for quite some time. As a perfectionist, this incident made me feel scarred, as though continuing to be the things I was before (a good student, hard worker, etc.) would never lead me to the same heights. I actually felt that everything I did from that point forward would be marked by this – like a gay permanent record of sorts.

Even worse than these feelings was the debilitating fear and anxiety I felt about whether or not what I had done would lead to me getting an STI or contracting HIV. Without having any gay friends, mentors, or role models, I was left to assess the situation using generalizations and stigma associated with the gay community. Society paints the gay community out to be deviant and promiscuous. Perhaps some of you can relate to the fact that I was even afraid to read up on the gay community because it felt like I was looking too deeply into something that I resented as possibly applying to me. I had my peripheral knowledge and fears – which were primarily fueled by random stereotypes from popular media. Hell, I didn't even know about the AIDS crisis because, sadly, you're not taught about that unless you seek the information out yourself.

Despite all of this, I was an anxious kid and studied the risks the best that I could before this meet up with Jason. Even with that knowledge, it's one thing to read advice online and a whole different story when the advice retroactively applies to something you already did. I replayed what happened that night over and over in my head. Did I do the risk factor on the 5th bullet of this list? *Did I?* What do they mean by "there's no verifiable proof that risk factor 4 won't get you HIV, but you never know and should get tested?" I hated the inconclusiveness, and I hated that I couldn't say that without a doubt I was at 0 risk for anything.

The issue was complicated by the fact that I didn't even know how I could get tested and what it entailed. There was no one else I felt comfortable to talk about it with – the whole point was that it needed to be secret. This was also a weird age – as many can relate – where you don't necessarily have your own adult doctor or money to get tested, and are completely intimidated by going to a free clinic in what is often the gayest part of town (the very thing you are avoiding associating yourself with and why you did this stupid sketchy thing to begin with.)

I remember for weeks I would just Google and read the same 14 articles about STI's and HIV, with slightly different inconclusive wordings that I would manipulate in my mind for a few hours to make me feel a bit more comfortable about what I did. "It is very unlikely that this poses a significant risk," my favorite article read. But it wasn't enough. I felt anxious and fearful every day. Did I do something irreversible? I felt I deserved it, if so. Perhaps that's exactly what society had taught me. I acted on what I shouldn't have, and I deserved everything coming to me.

Sadly, this is a feeling many gay men grapple with. The internalized idea that I deserved for something negative to happen amplified my fears. It would cosmically make sense that this stupid, awkward, and extremely short experience would somehow leave me with an STI or some other evidence of what I had done. Surely, if I acquired something through this and needed medication my parents would find out. I remember one day I was panicking during my commute and reading one of those 14 articles while driving in traffic. I actually got pulled over and received a ticket for being on my phone. The highway patrol solidified the strange metaphor for the entire experience – I was going to get caught for doing something wrong.

By this time, I felt nothing like myself. I lived in fear and anxiety – I cried most days. Eventually, I found a general diagnostic health facility near work that did anonymous STI testing using patient codes, rather than names. I didn't want to use school health insurance so none of it would be traceable. I paid what was probably several hundred dollars at the time to get my answers through a full testing panel. The days after this test actually provided no relief. Now, instead of fearing the unknown, I feared an automated phone call that would ask me for my patient code and then tell me whether or not I completely fucked up my life. It was a wonder I was able to go to work or school or be any amount of productive during the three-day span before I eventually got the call.

Of course, in true anxiety-ridden fashion, I did the math and realized it hadn't been four weeks since the hookup in my head. Four weeks, of course, is the time period that most of those 14 articles told me it takes for an HIV test to pick up a potential transmission with the greatest accuracy. My paranoid ass just spent hundreds of dollars to get tested in week 3, and I couldn't afford to do it again. I didn't know what to do.

The automated call finally came and I fumbled for my phone – my hands shaking as I cross-referenced the four digit patient code sealing my fate. Thankfully, the call blessed me with the knowledge that I was negative for everything. I felt slightly better that STI's were off the table, but the fear of even a low potential for HIV stuck with me for months to follow. I didn't get tested again for a very long time, and I can only imagine now how much anxiety that embedded in me until I ultimately got my reassurance. Anxiety continues to plague me in many areas of my life, undoubtedly amplified by this experience.

I wish I knew at that time what I do now about STI's, HIV,

medication, and an entire poz community leading extremely healthy and full lives. Only after beginning my journey of self-acceptance was I able to fully educate and protect myself in a healthier manner (both physically and mentally). It's troubling that the judgment of people outside of the gay community had so much influence over decisions that impacted my personal health. I hope that as more resources and awareness about the gay community come to light, subsequent generations don't have to feel so alone or afraid of something so normal. I think that's already beginning to happen in a way that didn't exist for me.

Taking stock of that entire experience, it makes me incredibly upset and sad that so many gay people had to (and still will) go through an ordeal similar to mine. You suppress your feelings toward the same sex for years out of fear of what it means and what the repercussions might be. After those years of internal torture, you finally act out on your desires to figure out if they're even real or feel good. Usually, this "acting out on your feelings" results in a completely disappointing and damaging experience that leads to further regret and anxiety.

These first experiences – at least in my case – fueled at least another year or two of complete suppression of desire toward the same sex. Every time I considered meeting or even talking to anyone online, I replayed that entire first experience in my head. How awkward and disappointing it was, how broken and empty I felt after, how fearful and anxious I was for the consequences, and how the whole thing made me feel "less than." Less than I was before, and completely incapable of going back to whom I used to be.

Ultimately, that first experience felt like a notch of disappointment in a figurative belt, and I feared that every subsequent experience would feel like a deeper notch squeezing me with pressure. That said, I knew I still couldn't get the idea that I may be gay out of my head. Despite how bad that first experience was, I knew that I still felt attraction toward men. The only difference was that it felt even worse and more confusing now, because I knew how I felt by acting out on my initial feelings. I had some verifiable proof of how horrible this potential "coming out" process might be for me. My first gay experience made me feel guilty and dirty for years. I am still chipping away at those feelings as an out man nearly a decade later.

What I didn't know at that time was that an app – Grindr – was just around the corner. Grindr was going to completely amplify the horrible experience I just went through. It was going to exponentially expand the amount of men available to me, and it was going to tell me how close they were in real time. It was going to bring hundreds of them to the palm of my hand at all times. It was going to give me endless options better than Jason.

Hundreds of men in the same position as me, hundreds of men more out than me, and hundreds of men more closeted than me. It was going to give me access to some of the hottest men that I had ever come across. It was going to give me access to men that I never imagined would be interested in the same sex. It was going to give me access to men who were dating and married to women. It was going to give me access to very successful men, and the many gorgeous men not doing shit with their lives. What I didn't know at that time was that just around the corner from all of the pain and regret of this experience was *this exact experience on steroids*. What was just around the corner was the Grindr grid, and these are my stories.

In part 2 of *The Grid*, I discuss three more impactful relationships involving Grindr in an attempt to unearth answers, extract lessons, and understand how even the earliest experiences from this app continue to impact me to this day.

[2] LESSON ONE: KAMRAN

It all started in law school, like so many other stressful endeavors. It was toward the latter half of a very difficult first year. The reasons for this were twofold: one, law school in general, and two, the fact that my first "secret gay relationship" had ended right before I began the school year, fueling the necessity for me to come out for my own sanity. It was an otherwise uneventful day of back-to-back lectures, sipping my Starbucks iced coffee and incessantly browsing Tumblr to maintain a touch point with the outside world. It was during this browsing in between lectures that we had unplanned class visit from a few students a grade year before us.

From time to time this would happen – older students or school administrators would come and talk to us about how difficult it was to pass the bar exam or why we needed to join a club to round out our "real world experience." I generally ignored these pleas since I had already been working in the industry for five years and knew that school's version of "real world experience" was more or less a joke compared to the actual "real world." No shade to extra curricular activities – get your experience, kids. There was an entirely different reason I looked up from the blue glow of Tumblr on my Macbook today.

There were two girls and a guy giving this speech, and I had never seen the guy before. I remember being instantly fixated on him. He had this aura about him that was nothing like I had come across before. For one, he was happy. Even in my nascent second year of LA living, I already knew this was rare to come across unless someone had literally hopped out of the plane/Hertz to follow his dreams. It was even more surprising to find this happiness in an LA law school environment, where dreams die (sorry, still a little burnt on the whole school experience). Beyond being happy, this guy also seemed so gregarious. He energetically explained whatever the fuck they were explaining to us, almost with a naïve and blissful ignorance about the work that goes into it. Honestly, I have absolutely no recollection of what they were telling us to do or join or contribute to. Perhaps the law review or some mock trial club.

I remember while the girls were explaining the exact same thing he was explaining (probably better, because women do everything better), I was just staring at him. I was hyper-analyzing every movement. Gay men tend to do this frequently. When we come across a new person, we analyze every word, movement, and visual cue to figure out if this person could possibly be playing for our team. How is he speaking, how is he carrying himself, what is he wearing, is he making a certain type of joke? Is there absolutely any reason that I have to fixate on this guy possibly being gay, because I want him. In other instances, you may just be figuring out whether or not you have a gay coworker, classmate, or if your girl friend's new man might be gay (it happens people – kind of a lot).

What I have glossed over here was just how handsome he was. He had the most beautiful smile. He was dressed relatively simply, but well. It was unclear if he had good style but things looked good on him. His clothes weren't too tight or loose, which of course left me with a big sexuality question mark. Not to fuel the idea that sexuality can be based on these generalizations – but sometimes guys intentionally send signals this way. There will always be a straight man in booty shorts to disprove me here – but you get what I'm saying. We work with the cues we receive. This guy also looked like he worked out (which was more important to me in this shallower phase of dating). He wasn't super built, but he looked like he worked out a few times a week for a realistically hot body. You know the one – "an ab could hypothetically be here, but I eat pizza instead – did you see my arm though?"

He was Middle Eastern, which has not historically been my type. Now if we're talking eight figures, *that's my type* (Saweetie, anyone?) Anyway, as an Armenian, I consider myself Middle Eastern (although I am upsettingly "white" for Census purposes), and have never felt a very close connection to my own people. It could be due to the fact that Middle Eastern people are some of the most repressed when it comes to sexuality, and for good reason when you see the repercussions of being gay in these countries. Even for American-born Middle Eastern kids, this culture of repression is so woven into families that most of the Middle Eastern men I meet are not out and have no plans to be anytime soon. It's a complicated and messed up dynamic where the "son of the family" is precious and revered, which amps up the extreme disappointment and perception of failure when that perfect male does the most unmanly thing – love another man. At the time, these generalized notions really biased me against men who looked like me.

This was all a heavier than intended way to convey to you that this was a very handsome Middle Eastern man in my class, and he had my complete attention. Of course, this moment was fleeting – and after a two-minute speech, this guy (lets call him Kamran) and his two partners were asking us if we had any questions. I didn't dare speak up, because I was honestly not even listening to their words and would have asked something stupid, but I hoped someone else did. I wanted any opportunity to drag this along and pick up on more cues from this guy.

Thankfully, I was in a class full of inquisitive know-it-alls, so a few people raised their hands. He spoke a bit more, I lusted a bit more, and then it was over. Everyone else immediately returned to

Facebook, Twitter, or online shopping for Victoria's Secret and BMW's (shout out to one of my favorite girls in class in front of me, if you ever read this). But I didn't immediately return to Tumblr. I sat there thinking about this guy, assigning some non-existent global meaning to what had just happened. Why did God choose this classroom – *my* classroom – to send this beautiful man? Why had I not seen him around before? Quick answers: because God sent him to every class and because he was a grade year older. But I didn't care – something about this person struck me in a profound way and I was determined to learn more.

Bi The Way

Within minutes, I had enlisted one of my only two friends in class at the time to a very important mission: "stalk the fuck out of Kamran until we figure out his sexuality" and – by the way – we will not accept straight as an answer. This was very much one of those "I don't care what *you* think your sexuality is" moments. They tend to happen when you are deeply mesmerized by someone in more than a "hot guy walking down the street" way. Perhaps you work with them, or they work at your doctor's office, or they make your coffee every morning. The people we have regular contact with but don't actually *know*. You start imagining who they are as a person, outside of their scrubs…naked. Kidding. But you know what I mean – knowing that you will see them more than once and being attracted to them, you start creating a story that meshes with your attraction and interest. We all want that non-existent gay rom-com love, and when even the slightest potential of it arises, we mentally fixate on making it happen.

To that point – this is one of the first men I met where Grindr was not the initial dick acquisition mechanism. Don't worry, this book is about Grindr and it most certainly comes into play later. But for this moment, I was so excited not to be using Grindr. If Kamran were gay, this would be a completely legitimate way to have met someone. This would be something I could tell my mom proudly one day. We crossed paths in legitimate ass school, in broad daylight, trying to better our damn futures. I suddenly felt like an elitist – oh, Grindr? I don't know her. I meet men through tasteful channels.

By now being an avid Grindr user, I found it amusing (but not surprising) that I was so quickly willing to jump ship, delete the app, and deny that I had ever used it. Something about Grindr – everything, actually – made me feel guilty at this time. It still felt wrong to be actively seeking men, even though I had recently come out to friends. It felt desperate. The few men I had met in the middle of the night in less than ideal (and less than safe) circumstances constantly affirmed the fact that I still felt best keeping this part of my life secret.

Ultimately, this was very much a valid stage of the gay experience – meeting and hooking up with men to figure out if this is even for you – but it felt very wrong compared to everyone else I knew in my life (primarily hetero) who had met far before apps existed via legitimate channels. School, work, and the oh so popular "through friends." I always thought, what are the damn odds of my friends having a friend that was handsome, out, 22 or so, and gay in the year of our lord 2012? Hell, even if they *did*, I wasn't ready for a relationship like that (despite what I thought). Grindr, unfortunately, was precisely the stage I was at – hoeish discovery.

Within 20 minutes my friend from class had some intelligence on Kamran. She tilted her Macbook toward me and pointed to a picture of him on Facebook, literally wearing a Pride t-shirt. It was a very short and anticlimactic investigation, but I was thrilled that we had our answer. After some more photos and group digging (are Facebook groups still a thing – I seriously haven't logged on since 2011), it became clear that Kamran might actually be bisexual. At this time I remember thinking, I will be more than happy to show him that he will ultimately be putting a ring on *this man's* finger. But bisexuality is, of course, a perplexing phenomenon in the gay community.

My perspective on bisexuality has changed quite a bit with time. Perhaps it has not been politically correct enough for me to post about on my blog, but this is a book so I feel I can get real without judgment, on the off chance that many can relate. When I was first considering coming out, bisexuality was actually a very attractive option for me. I figured, it's the best of both worlds and gives me a non-committal "out" from being gay, if I decide after a few dates and hookups that this just isn't for me. In a lot of ways, I think that "all or nothing" pressure of coming out is what is so debilitating for so many potentially gay men.

In those early stages, so many of us aren't necessarily hiding ourselves, but the idea that we will be forever marked as "gay" is something that seems difficult to turn back from. Perhaps it's because I, myself, had taken part to so many gossipy conversations along those lines. If I knew that someone had dated or hooked up with a man, and was later told that he was now dating a woman, I would very much be the ignorant person to say – "oh come on, he's gay – what's he trying to hide?" I guess it was only fair that the "people like that" in my mind were driving my own fear of being labeled forever gay, making it much more difficult to openly explore who I was. Karma is real. It was the great Lauren Conrad who once said *"You know what you did!"*

Nonetheless, bisexuality seemed like a viable option that would result in a less drastic label. I imagined people saying, "well he dated that *one* guy, but he was bisexual back then." Bisexual just had less of a sting than completely gay. But you notice I also said "back then." That is the second layer to my feelings on bisexuality. Back then, I very much saw it as a phase that all gay people go through. To an extent, I think this is partially valid, but I also (now) know that bisexuality is very real for a percentage of the LGBTQ+ population.

Back then, it made sense that many people went through a phase of exploration they labeled (at first) as bisexuality, out of the same non-committal fears I described. Once they figured out if they were actually gay or not, I assumed many of them dropped the bisexuality label and committed to whatever they actually felt they are. This is still likely true for some people, particularly those who come out a bit later in life and need additional time to explore feelings and instincts they may have ignored or didn't understand for some time. On the flip side, of course, I know a ton of people who just *knew* they were gay and were able to come out a very young ages without doubts or confusion. It is definitely a spectrum of experiences – but I certainly had strong (and unfair) perceptions of bisexuality.

When I found out that Kamran was bisexual, in addition to feeling a muddled agglomeration of everything I had just described – namely, whether or not this was just a phase or a real thing – I also felt a bit of hesitation. Sure, I had no idea what was even going to happen at this point, but I wondered, could I see myself with a bisexual person? At this time, I associated bisexuality with confusion. I assumed he was just in an unclear phase about whether or not he wanted to be with women or men, and had adopted a non-committal label to make his exploration easier to digest, perhaps for his family or cultural purposes.

Sure, coming out as bisexual is still difficult, but *not* coming out as gay gives the not-yet-accepting people in your life some hope to cling to and doesn't completely destroy relationships with some people who are adamantly against gays. When those people are your parents, buying a few years of "bisexual time" can make a huge difference. But I wondered, what would this mean for me? Would I constantly have to worry about him flirting with girls? Did he tell girls that he was bisexual, or would he only bring it up when he was dealing with a guy, to preserve that "straight" image?

I figured many women might actually be turned off if they found out that he also dated and slept with men. As an aside, I recently came across a post on the *Divorce Court* Instagram page posing that exact question – ladies, would you date a bisexual man? The results were overwhelmingly a judgmental variant of "hell no" – which is pretty sad. By the way, the *Divorce Court* page is amazing. Anyway, with Kamran, I felt that I could probably deal with him being bisexual, but not if that meant he rebranded his sexuality when convenient and advantageous to him.

I reflected back on the photo of him the Pride t-shirt – this wasn't a guy that was afraid of being his sexuality. The fact that this was publicly associated with his Facebook quelled a lot of my "what is he hiding" fears. Still, I wondered if he had ever been in a serious relationship with a guy and what the rules were. Was dating men a secondary, "fun" pursuit for him? Would he just hookup to fulfill a desire while he dated women more seriously to take home to mom? Was I potentially going to be someone's "only in the middle of the night?" All of these concerns were undoubtedly fueled by my own fear of bringing a guy home to a Middle Eastern mom (no matter how supportive parents are, it's a scary prospect).

This guy was very cute after all, and I knew that if he was cute to me he was also cute to the many women he encountered in the course of a day. Charming and light-hearted, I was positive that he got a lot of female attention. Would it be considered cheating on me if he flirted with women – or would it be considered a whole different avenue because it was a different gender? By now I knew that gay men were already hard to pin down and trust, and I was extremely worried that I had to think about an additional gender coming for my man...who wasn't actually mine at all.

My views on bisexuality have since matured quite a bit. Having spent a number of years as an out gay man, I often reflect back on the idea or potential that I could have been bisexual after all. Did I give it enough of a chance, did I miss out on exploring a different side of myself? Honestly, no. Sexuality is truly a spectrum and however you choose to identify along it at any point in time is completely up to you. Nothing has ever stopped me from exploring that. Heterosexuality, bisexuality, and homosexuality are all equally valid permanent or fluid states.

Without a doubt there are people who will be straight, bi, or gay for the rest of their lives. There are people who will be straight and later come out as gay, bi and later come out as gay, and even gay that might later go back to bi or straight. It is not anyone's position to dictate how another feels and identifies on this spectrum. They are all valid experiences. I sometimes feel that it is unfair to bisexual people – "real" bisexual people – that so many gay people use bisexuality as a phase. But I realize that *that* is wrong too. Whether permanent or temporary, everyone's experience with bisexuality is real at that point in time. It's not fair to say some people are "using" it when it is simply just how they identified on a spectrum at a point in time. No one would ever tell someone that was assumed to be straight for 20 years who later came out as gay – "wow, you disrespected the straight experience by faking it for 20 years."

Perhaps bisexuality is more debated since it is a relatively newer (public) phenomenon than heterosexuality. Of course, it has existed for ages – we are just talking about it more. That said, if you are beginning to date a bisexual person, I think it is completely fair to respectfully ask them questions about their sexuality that will help you better understand their feelings, needs, and desires. These are the types of questions we should be asking any potential partner, regardless of sexuality. I think if I were patient and straightforward enough to have an honest discussion with Kamran about these topics (when the time was right), it would have suppressed a lot of my concerns. Unfortunately, without the benefit of years of additional perspective, Kamran received the detriment of my confusion and skepticism regarding bisexuality.

You Belong With Me

With extreme lust – and uncertainty – I began plotting how I would potentially approach Kamran. Although I knew that he was open to men, I had no idea if he was single and how to get into contact. I quickly realized that meeting people the "legitimate" way and not on Grindr was challenging. On Grindr, at the very least, you know the person is gay, online, and whether he's supposed to be or not, is open to receiving messages and probably dating or hooking up with you.

In the real world, every step of that is a mystery. All I had to go off of was the Pride picture and this speech he had given to the class.

So, in the corniest way possible, I e-mailed his *school* e-mail, and said that I was really interested in the club he was pitching and had a few questions I wanted to ask him. Perhaps we could meet up really quickly between classes to discuss. I included my phone number after my name, as if it was something I included with every e-mail. Let's be real, I just sent it to open the door to texting. Of course, I had absolutely no interest in that damn club and – honestly – he probably didn't either. If he were legitimately involved in this law review (or whatever it was), he would be explaining it a lot more miserably because that stuff is very difficult. He struck me as being a part of it because – on paper – it looks good and is what you're supposed to do. Maybe he helped write one article or was on the team for moral support, but I knew he was not your typically invested, over-achieving student.

I remember being extremely nervous about this e-mail. Even though it was very purposefully not flirtatious, for me, this was one of the first times I was putting myself out there in a more public way than the orange cocoon of Grindr. Presumably, he was going to respond to this e-mail, and I was going to have to meet him and continue this charade of caring about this club or somehow turn this into a more flirtatious endeavor. "What the hell are you getting yourself into," I wondered. On the other hand, I couldn't stop thinking about this guy, and in other areas of life – work, school – I was very much a "bitch if you want it you can get it" type of person.

I must have wanted this for me to be going this far, so I was determined to get it. Only several hours after my e-mail, I received a response from Kamran. There is something so exciting about that unread dot on iPhone e-mail. Usually, when it's a job offer but in this case, when it is coming from your formerly anonymous suitor. As the e-mail loaded, I imagined the response possibilities. "Yes – let's talk about it," or maybe, "fuck the club I looked your pretty ass up on Instagram what are you doing later?" It was not the latter, but it was better than I expected. He said he would definitely answer any questions I had, and even offered his phone number in return to make things quicker or facilitate meeting up.

Oh shit. I had some traction. This whole thing definitely could have been handled over e-mail, really, but he was down to either meet or text about it. I wondered if he looked me up somehow and already had developed his own interest in me. Hell, he's just super polite and naïve, I reasoned that he probably *actually* thinks I want to know about this damn club. At any rate, I took the bold step of texting him – "hey, it's Lex from the e-mail – when is a good time to meet-up on campus?" And so it began.

We began texting back and forth, but not about the club or setting up a time to meet. Don't get me wrong, it wasn't immediately flirtatious, but we did an above board exchange about classes, finals, and other general ranting about the law school experience. He was curious about the particular program I was in and how stressful it was, so it opened the door to a broader conversation. One way or another, we got to talking about his roommate, who is also Armenian, which he asked me about either because of my last name or because he had a lot of Middle Eastern friends and just knew. When I finally connected who his roommate was in my mind, my heart dropped. Admittedly, I know very few Armenians outside of my family, but I immediately recalled who his roommate was.

Somebody That I Used To Know

At the very beginning of the school year, when I was first using Grindr after the break up of my "secret gay relationship" (I keep referencing it – maybe it should be it's own book one day when I have a couple years of free time to write), I had an exchange with Kamran's somewhat closeted gay roommate. The exchange didn't go well. I was excited when I was first speaking to his roommate, based off of a blurry and cropped photo. I found out that he was Armenian *and* in law school. *My* law school, actually, which I did not confirm to him at that point in an attempt to protect my privacy. In a way, it was a less prestigious iteration of the same excitement I had with Kamran. Even though we were speaking on Grindr, I figured – wow, if I could land an Armenian lawyer this whole gay thing would be a lot easier for my parents to stomach.

I probably chatted with this guy for a few hours before he sent me more photos of himself. You know how this goes. It was a shallower time, but I have to keep it real in permanent print. He just wasn't my type – and I probably didn't message this in as mature of a way as I can probably manage these days. I was pretty disappointed, because I was excited to be talking to him, but such are the risks of a blurry-cropped photo guy talking to another blurry-cropped photo guy. Not being out on Grindr is a crapshoot. I probably said something along the lines of "sorry man, not my type." Not necessarily evil, but not necessarily crafted to make the other person feel better, especially after hours of vibing via good conversation. It was abundantly clear that my ultimate decision on him as a person was ruined by how he looked, and that just isn't cool. Of course, his reaction was dramatic, as they tend to be. Something along the lines of a "really man? Fuck you."

I've written about this before online, but the whole "not my type" experience can be much improved. Rejecting on dating apps is a necessary evil, and people cannot be beholden to talk to and date people they have no physical chemistry with. There are hundreds, even thousands, of guys we are exposed to on these things. Unless you're some sex and love robot, you are not going to be right for a vast majority of them and may need to reject from time to time. Everyone is going to reject, and be rejected often – it's just how it goes. Accordingly, I think the best policy is to be polite – something along the lines of "you are cute and I think we connect on a lot, but unfortunately you are not the usual type I go for."

I think saying "you are not my physical type," or something similar, implies that the person is out of shape or not fit enough for you. Whether or not that is actually your reason (come on body queens supporting *The Grid*, but really, stop being shallow!) saying "usual type" seems a bit less harsh. "Usual type" implies that for whatever reason, there is a type of guy you are attracted to, and although this person is attractive, he just isn't what you go for. For the person being rejected – which again, is all of us at one point or another, it's best not to take these things personally and just move on. "It's been nice chatting – hope you find someone right for you." Getting upset or feeling personally devalued by this experience means you are taking it too seriously, and while it's important to do so, you need to build a bit of tolerance with the high volume of apps like Grindr so you don't lose your actual mind.

To bring this full circle – here I was texting Kamran, facing the realization that I had "sorry bro – not my type-ed" his damn roommate. My mind immediately went racing. Is he going to ask his roommate about me or did he already? Is his roommate his best friend? This was awkward. In the vast universe of LA gays, I am now dealing with two of them, who live together and go to the same school as me. Geolocation had officially failed me.

I managed to maneuver around the potentially awkward moment by downplaying it. Something like, "hmm – who is your roommate? I think we may have spoken on Grindr very briefly, I don't really remember." Whether or not he would ask the roommate and determine I was a horrible person was up in the air, but I made it past an uncomfortable hurdle. What I did accomplish – and consciously so – was dropping the fact that I knew of and used Grindr in this first conversation. It was a risky move, but hey, I figured if he could live with a roommate actively seeking men online, he must be cool with this gay thing (despite his still ambiguous bisexuality). Maybe he even used Grindr himself, or wanted to explore it. In fact, what I was really doing was driving home the fact that I was definitely gay and single.

I think he said something like "*oh* Grindr," as if to confirm that it was not a foreign concept and something he may have used himself. Suddenly, in less than a 24 hour period, I had gone from "OMG is it possible that this guy is even gay" in class, to literally texting him about our mutual understanding of Grindr. What a quick turnaround – and how convenient that his Grindr-using roommate facilitated this discussion and helped us bypass probably weeks of awkward figuring things out.

A short time later, Kamran asked if I had time to meet up for lunch or dinner between classes or studying that week. You know – to discuss my "questions about the club." Of course, we both knew that we had some general and potentially flirtatious rapport – not to mention an ability to openly discuss Grindr, so the possibilities were endless. By now, I assumed this was going to be some version of a date, but if it went horribly or if I completely misread the situation, I could quickly turn it around to a general meeting with a kid from school. He could be a cute friend, at worst. The tricky part of this all was that we were right up against finals week, which seriously requires you to put everything aside and study (aka memorize things) like crazy. For some reason, he wasn't too worried about it, and I had to eat anyway – so I agreed to meet him for dinner the next night.

The Boy Is Mine

I went to the school library that next day for a full day of studying. I was prepared to go from library to dinner, so I showed up in my "date beat." At this time, that typically meant jeans, v-neck, backwards hat, and grande iced coffee in hand to convey that "I'm a busy and caffeinated bitch, make this worth my time." I continued texting Kamran throughout the day (via iMessage on my laptop – quite distracting to the studying process). He was doing his own version of studying, from home. People tended to ramp up studying a day or two before their actual tests, so I think he had more leeway before his finals than I did.

Eventually it was time to meet up downtown. I offered to pick him up from his place, which was literally between school and the restaurant. Even though I hadn't been on hundreds of dates at this point in my gay experience (which, sadly, I cannot say anymore), I did know that offering to pick up a guy is a huge risk. If the date goes horribly wrong or if he is completely awkward, you're on the hook for driving them home. This was literally right before Uber, people – put yourself in these prehistoric times. But I also figured, this was different. This wasn't some random Grindr meet-up you leave in the dust if something goes wrong. We go to the same school, and this was kind of sort of not even a date, so it's just meeting someone from school. But why are we meeting at night – at a restaurant? Bitch, this was a date. But he's so fucking cute, how badly could it go? I concluded that I would have to drive his insufferable cute ass home regardless of what happened.

I pulled up to his parking garage – two minutes early – and texted him that I was just about to pull up. Early and playing it cool, as always. He texted that he would be right down. To his credit, it was a colossal apartment complex, but this was my first brush with Kamran reality. As I sat and waited, 3 minutes, 6 minutes, 8 minutes…I got very confused and texted him. "Hey – am I in the right spot?" To me, when someone says they'll be right down, we're talking 3-5 minutes maximum. Another 2 minutes passed before he responded. "Am I being flaked on?" I wondered. How awkward would that be to bring me to your front door to do something like this. Was this an elaborate plan with the roommate I had rejected to get me back? Were they both going to come down and confront me? It only takes several minutes for my mind to go into conspiracy mode. Meanwhile, his building's security guard was eyeing me with the "you have about 30 seconds before I come tell you to move out of this driveway" stare.

Kamran told me he was just finishing getting ready. I was like – are you actually serious? You knew about this date (or whatever this is) all day, we've been talking all day, this is when I said I'd pick you up, and your ass is still not ready. I tried to be patient, but younger me had a short fuse for these men wasting my time. But this wasn't some random Grindr meet up. I had actively pursued this guy, and was genuinely excited and very nervous to meet him. I want to say he finally came downstairs in the 15-20 minute stretch after my original arrival. I could begrudgingly tolerate this from one of my girl friends, but come on, how long did it literally take you to put on this borderline ill-fitted t-shirt and hat?

But there was something about how that stupid t-shirt and hat looked on him that immediately made you forget that you were upset. This guy was charming, and he knew it, and he used it to get away with things. I knew this much already. He basically should have said "sorry I'm late, but I'm really cute and smile a lot so you can't stay mad at me for more than 20 seconds." I'm like a puppy that just chewed your Louboutin. You hate me but you won't do shit about it. He was right. I was over my anger approximately 45 seconds into our drive to the restaurant. It also helped that I was nervous about this whole thing.

There was a weird dynamic in the air. You were this unattainable and perfect being a couple days ago, and now you're in my car like the many Grindr dates of yore. I didn't know which version of myself to be – Grindr Lex or school Lex. They were distinctly different people. Grindr Lex was a bit more fun, more LA, knew what he wanted. School Lex was way more serious, anxious, and professional – not ideal for a pseudo-date. I struck a still uncomfortable compromise toggling between both personalities, which probably made me seem weird to him for quite a while. I was nervous, and I typically wasn't nervous on Grindr dates because the stakes were so low. I was nervous for hookups, for sure, but an initial date in the public didn't really scare me much. This was different; I had a lot of assumptions to clarify and a personal romantic agenda to carryout.

I needed to steer this from a meeting about school to a date, fairly quickly. He looked cute, but also casual, which didn't give me much clarity on whether or not this was a date. For gay men in LA, t-shirt was very much an acceptable date look, but *more* than a t-shirt also happened from time to time and made it super clear that the guy was trying. So here we were, in our best "date t-shirts" wondering if these were "romantic t-shirts" or "this was the only clean one I had" t-shirts. He chose a restaurant in Little Tokyo that didn't serve Japanese food. I would soon learn that choices like that were very much Kamran – nothing quite made sense.

The dinner was pretty damn awkward. He was cuter than I remembered, and it was messing with my confidence. I kept thinking that he was only hanging out with me to give me advice about school, or get some intelligence about his roommate's Grindr antics. For some reason, I felt like I wasn't worthy of someone as cute he was. It would be too perfect – this handsome guy who is proudly into guys from the same school – it couldn't work. In between the awkwardness, I did manage to slide in a few jokes and sarcastic comments that grabbed his interest. I feel like he must have felt I was cute too, and at the very least, witty.

In a surprising move (even to me), I decided to bring up his roommate. I was tired of talking about school and faking interest in the damn club that led to us crossing paths. I knew bringing up his roommate would open up the conversation to Grindr, and potentially, what he's doing with his sexuality and what he's looking for. After all, we could still be here as two friends ranting about how hard it is to find a guy in LA. My strategy worked like a charm, and I learned a lot.

For one, it seemed like he wasn't as close to his roommate as I thought. He didn't know much about his roommate's private Grindr endeavors, and confirmed that he didn't ask his roommate about me. I was relieved, and even admitted that his roommate wasn't my type so I hoped that I wasn't too rude to him. Kamran seemed to understand, as if to imply that *he* was the cuter roommate in the house. I asked if he had much time for dating with school and the club and everything. He said he tried from time to time. By now, we had discussed at least the potential that he had used Grindr before, so I felt comfortable asking if he dated more women or men, or how it all worked.

He seemed right in the middle – open to dating either and did so somewhat regularly, but had not had a long-term relationship for a while. To his credit, he did mention a couple of relationships that lasted several months, with a couple women and a guy, which was a strong showing for being in your early 20's in LA. I thought wow – maybe this guy is into consistency and finding something serious. At the very least, maybe the twisted allure of a hookup with a new guy every night (and next-day STD test) wasn't for him. It did seem, in fact, that he had a vision of a long-term connection in his head. He mentioned that he came out to his parents as bisexual, but that they weren't thrilled about it and didn't discuss it much. A typical reaction and state of affairs for Middle Eastern families. But the idea of "bringing someone home" that they approved of seemed important to him. I didn't push him on if or how that would ever be a guy.

Despite hating the food, the dinner turned around a bit. We were becoming more open and comfortable talking. Eventually, this enabled me to ask about the "elephant in the room." I said something like "so did you think we were really going to talk about the club when I reached out to you?" He admitted that at first he *did* think so, but based on all of our texting and when the conversation was going, he suspected things could go in a different direction. I asked, then – was this a date? "Do you want it to be?" he offered. I said "sure – why not?" Always playing it cool, I was officially in Grindr Lex mode. We were officially on a date – and I was pleased with how quickly I had gotten exactly what I wanted.

Just Hold On...

We decided to walk around after the dinner, and to no one's surprise (if you've been reading these stories or know me irl), we ended up at a Starbucks down the street. I told him I was no good without a constant iced coffee in my hand. The line was pretty long, so we were standing there for at least 5 minutes. Kamran used this time to bring up a conversation we had at dinner. It was about just how *out* both of us were. At dinner, I told him I was out to friends and regularly dating guys so I felt relatively comfortable with myself. I guess since he was a year or two older and out to his family, he felt superior in his "outness." He decided to take the opportunity to test me, and really gauge whether or not I was ready to publicly date a guy.

He asked what I would do if he held my hand – right here in line. I instantly freaked out. Sure I was *out* to the people I felt comfortable telling, and sure, I went on dates with guys in public, but in that moment, he confronted me with the fact that I wasn't as out as I thought. I guess on all of my dates with guys, I felt comfortable in that from the outside looking in, we could have looked like two male friends grabbing coffee or a bite to eat. We weren't holding hands or making out or touching – we were just being two people in public. Whomever I was with knew it was a date, but potentially no one else did. I realized that gave me a level of comfort in these early exploration days, and Kamran was putting me to the test. I absolutely hated how it made me feel. I really liked him and suddenly I was in a do-or-die scenario. It felt like if I didn't hold his hand right now, it would prove to him that I'm not as out as I need to be to be his boyfriend.

No one should be pushed beyond their comfort zone in relationships, but I guess it is a natural reality to be dating people that are more or less out than you, especially as young gay men. I also considered the repercussions, now and in general. I generally didn't like the idea of holding hands in public as gay men, because you immediately become a potential target. Especially in crowded areas like downtown, or a movie or concert – there is always a drunk (or, hell, completely sober) homophobic bro with 2 or 3 of his friends ready to call you out and potentially get very aggressive. "Why would we make ourselves a target?" I wondered. I generally sought a peaceful and anti-violent existence, and holding hands unfortunately seemed to put that in danger.

Sadly, I still feel the same way to this day, and I know that many gay people relate. You constantly have to monitor your surroundings and assess whether or not a gesture of affection – kissing, hugging, or holding hands – is going to put you at risk for some sort of judgment or attack. Do we really need to show each other affection at this *exact moment*, you often wonder. To be clear, I had no problem doing this stuff (even back then) in the privacy of a home or car – but being in public totally threw me off. I applaud and even envy the gay people that are comfortable doing these things whenever and however they choose. You all are really pushing the needle forward on the fact that same-sex affection should be acceptable in public to the same extent that heterosexual affection is. Maybe I am personally not a PDA person, regardless of sexuality. Maybe I will feel more comfortable as same-sex affection is normalized over time. But here, in this Starbucks, on this day, I had no idea what to do.

Against my will, I just did what he wanted to keep this going. He held my hand. "Who the fuck holds hands in the Starbucks line?" I wondered. This is uncomfortable and unnatural. It would have been one thing if it was a special moment, and he squeezed my hand, and it meant something. But the fact that he positioned it as "are you gay enough to hold my hand right now in front of these baristas and randoms" took away from it. Regardless of how uncomfortable it was, I was surprised that it felt kind of nice. I was scared, and it felt unnatural, but just to connect with him – touch – and have him squeeze my hand suddenly brought us closer. Perhaps it was artificially closer, but I was very much that middle school girl – "oh my God, he's touching me." It lasted for only a brief moment, but a few seconds more than I expected. I thought we were doing it in a 3-second-dare type fashion, but he really wanted to test me. This was a 10-15 second hand hold situation. In the end, it was an equal mix between nice and uncomfortable, and he should have had more tact about the entire situation.

Public displays of affection can be quite triggering to gay people. Perhaps someone has had a negative experience before where they were targeted, or perhaps they just aren't at that stage of their sexuality. It would seem to be fair to have a conversation with the person before engaging in anything that they aren't ready for. Sure, it is potentially awkward to have a talk about holding hands – as it is admittedly more special when it just happens naturally, but there are ways to work around it. Perhaps hold hands for the first time in a somewhat private yet public moment – during a movie, in a park, in a secluded spot on the beach. Maybe after that first time you can ask – or just have a natural feel – for how comfortable your partner is with those things. Regardless, please never do what Kamran did. Please never *test* someone's sexuality by pressuring them into a public display of affection. We deal with enough judgment, fear, shame, and confusion as a community, we do not need to amplify it for one another with this sort of one-upping of sexuality.

...We're Going Home

After a bit more walking and talking, we got into my car. I recalled how I was potentially nervous about hating him in this moment and begrudgingly completing the drive home, but that wasn't the case. Many aspects of him threw me off – but I did still think he was adorable. Honestly, after this first date (I would classify it as such after the hand holding debacle), I felt much less threatened by him. He wasn't as intimidating as I'd thought – he actually seemed a bit naïve and harmless. He wasn't some smartass law student, he was a normal ass guy trying his best. He seemed to fall into the role due to the pressures of a Middle Eastern family and successful siblings.

You would think I could relate, but no one actually pushed me into law. I guess I had a lot more self-awareness and maturity than he, for being a bit younger. I suddenly perceived Kamran as a project. He was very cute, and presented some red flags, but all in all I felt like (what I assume to be) the typical girl when she meets a man she likes. He has some issues, but I like some other things, so I will make him my project, recognizing that this will take a lot of "training."

I remember at this time I would often shuffle all of my music during car rides, leaving the potential for a one-off Arabic song to come on that I downloaded as homage to my childhood. My parents loved listening to Arabic music. Of course, an Arabic song came on and I had an "oh fuck – skip it quick" this is embarrassing moment. Kamran turned it up and started dancing. I was like *who* is this guy? Celebrating the very things I hide about myself to homogenize and fit in. I was a bit envious that he seemed so much freer than me in this sense, and it attracted me quite a bit to him.

I pulled up to his building's driveway, the same security guard staring. It was time for the awkward goodbye. Do we kiss? Do we hug? Do we do a weird in-car bro-hand-slap-with-the-quarter-hug-thing? The last two being a recurring conundrum for most gay men meeting *any* other men – to be honest. I didn't have much time to agonize – he quickly kissed me on the cheek and said he would talk to me later. He walked up into his building, and I sat there for a second. This bold motherfucker – he's just out here kissing bitches, no questions asked. Something that I would have stressed about for several dates, he just did like it was nothing. Again, I was left both envious of how comfortable he seemed with himself and attracted to him for it. What did he mean by "later," I wondered? Later tonight? Did he mean "soon?" I remember feeling a bit worried about how invested he was. I felt like I was going to have to text *him* to keep this going, which is an unfortunate feeling.

Reciprocation is a tough topic in dating, and gay dating is no exception. Most people fully recognize when reciprocation is not happening appropriately. For instance, let's say you had a solid first date, like I would say happened here with Kamran. You like him, and you hope he likes you back. Some hallmarks of this would be communicating after the date was over *that same night*. One of you may say "I had a great time – hope to see you again soon." Ideally, it's always the other person and not you, solidifying their interest in you. Often, that is not the case or you're just not patient enough to wait. You don't want to play games and don't mind identifying your continued interest first. In that case, you put yourself out there and hope for reciprocation. If you receive it, you are instantly validated. If you don't immediately receive, you begin the hyper-analyzation process.

Without reciprocation, most of us make global assessments (often inaccurate) about what went wrong with this person, or what must wrong with us for this not to have worked?

"I knew it – I was so awkward – I suck at social interaction."

"I knew it – I'm not good looking enough to sustain his interest."

"I knew it – my pictures were too filtered and he hated my acne and flabby stomach."

"I knew it – I wasn't smart enough to go out with a scientist."

The list is unfortunately endless. Now, if the guy texts back a couple hours later, we immediately stop our analyzing. "Oh – never mind I'm not ugly – he was just busy." What if he doesn't text until the next day? You begin wondering...

"Well, what time does he work?"

"I check my phone for texts when I wake up, why wouldn't he?"

"Does he have a job that enables him to text, or is this a put your phone in this locker until your break situation?"

"Does his car have Apple CarPlay? How hard would it have been to dictate a "nice meeting you?" on his way to work? He hates me."

Because our hearts and feelings are involved, we often fail to make more practical assessments of reciprocation (or a lack thereof). I always wonder why this is the case, since in the high-volume world of online dating, a lack of reciprocation is a perfectly normal (and expected) state of affairs. Why can't more of us take a step back from the situation and say "ok – he didn't text me and honestly, based on that date, I would say we have some differences in personality that would be challenging to overcome." Perhaps this is only easy to do when we deem the person as equally or less attractive than ourselves. It's almost like you're not losing anything, because who you met was a dime a dozen, and can eventually be found again in a more compatible form.

But what about when we perceive the person as more attractive than us? We might perceive someone as our "dream man" or "soul mate," words that are often thrown around far too early in dating. When *those* guys don't respond, our internalized feelings about ourselves and how worthy we are (or aren't) suddenly come to the surface. When this mythical "hot" guy agrees to go on a date with us, it feels like a job interview at your dream job. We assign all of the power to the other person, and they can make or break our future by deciding to pursue us. If they decide against us, we aren't good enough for some reason.

But what if we approached dating these "mythical" figures more pragmatically? At the end of the day, being nervous or constantly reminding yourself that someone is "too good for you" can be a self-fulfilling prophecy. Regardless of appearance, people are generally attracted to a certain level of confidence and self-awareness – knowing who you are and proudly displaying it. This is your best chance at any date – and I don't care who you're meeting, they shouldn't detract from your confidence.

After a date with a "mythical" figure, you should remain steadfast in your self-perception. If you really liked him, go ahead and reach out (once) and put yourself out there. If they respond, great. If not, they might not have been right for you. It's not about you as a person, or whether or not you were good enough for this particular person. Do not devalue yourself to a level that pins your entire self-worth on whether or not some random hot guy is going to respond to your text. If I may: Almost. All. Of. These. Hot. Men. Ain't. Shit. Sure, there are one-offs, but I firmly believe that the hotter you are, the further I have to dig to find your flaws because God is fair – and she doesn't just make perfect people. Here's a little trick for being dumped, ghosted, or left on read by a hot person. *Remember* that you are almost always dodging a bullet. If it is hard to get that first response from them, you have a long road ahead. A road full of perpetual waiting, analyzing why they do what they do, and whether or not they like you. It is a very frustrating and unhealthy relationship dynamic.

In general, and outside of this "mythical hot guy" hypothetical, use reciprocation as a tool in your favor rather than to tear yourself down. If reciprocation happens, you are at the very least dealing with someone equally interested and should explore the relationship if you would like to (also, if you don't like someone, it's very nice to reciprocate and at least let them know how you feel so they don't have to agonize over it.) If reciprocation does not occur, mentally thank the person for saving your time – because if they don't like enough about you right off the bat to respond to a simple call or message, they did not recognize your value. That's not to say there aren't one-offs who inadvertently forget to reciprocate, but I feel like the consideration of one-offs is what gets people stuck on men who don't reciprocate for far too long.

"Well, he's in school, so he has long nights and forgets to text." "Well, he goes surfing so his phone is probably in the car or at the bottom of the ocean." "Well, he's going through some family stuff so he probably forgot to respond." No sister – I guarantee you in 99% of examples you give me – short of "in surgery" or "death of immediate family member" – the person most definitely had their phone, saw the message, and didn't respond in a reasonable amount of time simply because it is not a priority for them. *He's just not that into you* is most often the answer, and that's something that we need to reframe as a fair reality, and not a statement on our self-worth. Remind yourself that "I'm still a bad bitch, just not *your* bad bitch, and that's fine because whoever is right for me will recognize my value and reciprocate."

<u>Kiss Kiss</u>

Unfortunately, I did not have the benefit of this advice after the date with Kamran. I tried to play it cool and waited about an hour or so after the date to shoot him a text. Of course he had sent me nothing in the interim. I said something like – "hey – that was a fun night, hope we can hang out again." To drive the point home to you all, I was very attracted to him and very much hanging onto this dream of dating someone from law school, despite our potential differences. Approximately two hours later – and yes, you can imagine my hyper-analyzing and agonizing in between – he sent a short text to affirm the same. "Yeah – we should hang out sometime soon man." It was a bit short, and vague. Did he mean he only wanted to continue as classmates and friends, or did he actually have romantic interest? What about that goodbye peck – was that something he did with everyone? I wouldn't put it beyond him – he was a charmer, after all. What did he mean by "man" – was that his equivalent of "bro?" Were we bros now – is this how bisexual people talk? I would come to find out all of these answers over a very confusing, exciting, and frustrating few weeks of interacting with Kamran.

We continued texting the next day, but a little less frequently than before we had met. As it tends to go, things often get hot and heavy via text before you meet someone. You have the benefit of building an image of them in your mind that conforms to exactly what you desire. Their words via text help you piece together a mental image, and those words often don't even need to be very good. If you have built in your head that you are texting some guy from Grindr that is your personal Frank Ocean, all he really has to do is text back "yup" every few hours for you to freak out over how mysterious and sensitive he is.

But as soon as you meet someone in person, you face some sobering realities. They don't look like you remember, or you didn't imagine them at this height. They only talk about themselves and can't reciprocate a single question. Their voice is nerdy – you were imagining something more suave. So many things can go wrong when you move from digital fantasy to reality. That has always been an issue with meeting men online – it is never what it seems. You can try to bypass some of this with phone calls and FaceTime prior to meeting, but those are often met with objection as some people feel like what is a casual conversation suddenly becomes a job interview for your affection. It saves everyone a lot of time and also acts as an additional layer of safety, confirming you are speaking to who you thought you were – but I can appreciate the concerns and potential for judgment on both ends.

I knew that something about me in reality did not add up to what may have been Kamran's digital fantasy of me. Of course, we had crossed paths in person, but the first time we spoke directly was by e-mail and text. He may have looked up a photo, and used that as a base, but something went wrong on that date. He was clearly still open to exploring the relationship, but once again, I felt the balance had tilted back in his favor. I seemed to want this just a little bit more than him, and accordingly, had to do more of the heavy lifting when it came to communication. I didn't back away from the challenge – I never seemed to do so when it involved me getting what I want. "I just need to get him in my corner," I thought. Once he definitely wants *me*, then I can make the decision about whether or not I want *him*. These games and power dynamics are quite common in gay dating. There are a lot of egos involved.

I recall on a couple occasions we met up on campus between classes. This always made me feel a bit uncomfortable, because the campus was very small. Everyone knew everyone, perhaps not personally, but enough to assign a mental note. "That's the guy that smokes a cigarette outside at 8:30 AM every morning in the blue jacket." If he's not there, something is wrong. I was in a small program within the school, so I was literally always with my class of 30 or so people every day. If any one of us was missing, suddenly hanging out with new people, or not doing a certain thing at a certain time – people noticed. I wondered if other people knew about

Kamran's sexuality – after all, he wore that Pride shirt all the time. Even though I was out to my friends, I didn't necessarily want to publicly be out to my entire school. I wondered if by virtue of being seen with him all the time, people might connect the dots. The reality was our schedules were quite different – so it was never a big issue.

The closest call was when we once met on the school's back patio area. I had never gone there before, in nearly an entire year of being a student. It wasn't some secret, but unless you wanted to eat your lunch or chill at a moldy picnic table– you didn't really need to be back there. Frankly, I liked to show up to school and get the hell out as soon as it was over. I remember he asked me to meet him back there, and I told him that my next class started in a few minutes. I was already sitting inside. It would take me another couple minutes to get to where he was. He kept urging me to go. I kept denying him. Precious minutes were passing by. Finally, I said "fuck it" – let me go over there and make him feel guilty for making me late, at the very least.

I met him, and he looked like a harmless puppy, as usual. Suddenly, I wasn't annoyed anymore. He just wanted to ask how my day was going. We caught up for a few minutes, but I told him I really needed to get back to class. He let me go, but not before he surprisingly kissed me. Another "oh shit" middle school girl moment ensued. It was so spontaneous, but I was also completely terrified. I hadn't scanned the area around me for others. It seemed pretty private – but you never know. I wondered if anyone was looking out there from the windows. I just had another PDA moment with this guy against my will. It felt very weird, but again, nice. It kind of made me feel like I was his. What were these mixed signals? Sure, we text a lot, and hang out sometimes, but now we kiss between classes? Am I your boyfriend or am I one of your many side pieces? I walked back upstairs, slower than I thought I would. The moment kept running through my mind. I came into class and everyone stared at me, as I was several minutes late, which had never happened before. I sat down and just stared ahead of me for a few minutes with the scarlet ass letter on my laptop. Something was happening here.

Are You *That* Somebody?

Over the next few weeks, we continued to spend time together. Not every day, but more frequently. We would usually meet at coffee shops in and around Koreatown. At the very least, we always had homework in common, so it was an excuse to be productive but also around each other. I slowly learned more about him. Although he seemed to take school mostly seriously, I felt like he was much less invested than me. I often asked him how much work he had to do, and he would tell me, then I would watch him be completely distracted at the coffee shop while I actually did my work. How does he ever finish, I wondered. Realistically, he probably didn't.

He seemed to slide by and do the bare minimum and hope for the best. Even though he had a year or two on me by age, I solidly felt much more mature. I often felt like an older brother or dad, telling him his approach to things wasn't realistic. I remember when he was looking for a summer internship, I asked him about his process. Again, very half-assed. He didn't seem to have a strong interest in any particular legal area, and I wondered if any of this was for him. He struck me as someone that would eventually regret going to law school and fall into something completely unrelated.

One of our early dates really drove home our incompatibility. We met for coffee in Larchmont Village (his choice), a cute little street of shops and restaurants in the middle of LA. I didn't often go there, as I was a utilitarian dater in these days. Cute dates were for the second or third time meeting someone (if that ever happened). Let's just meet at the closest Starbucks and figure out if this is even a thing worth planning for. I don't need flower arrangements on the tables and an up and coming actress as a waitress. Not very romantic, but a convenient approach to high volume dating. I had been to

Larchmont before, but remember thinking this is pretty damn cute –
he must like me or at least take me seriously. Otherwise, he took all
his hoes here.

We sat on a picturesque back patio and just talked. Seriously
talked on a deeper level than before. More than just how school
went or how annoying things were, but about things like politics
(generally bad date topic, people) and culture. Looking back, I felt
that Kamran was often testing me to see if I was good enough for
him. I feel like he had a checklist in his mind – maybe I met some
needs but not others, so the early days felt like a constant test. Here,
I felt like he was testing if I was smart or cultured enough for him,
perhaps he was used to a cuter and shallower type when it came to
men in LA. Of course, within minutes of deep discussion, I realized
he just liked to hear himself talk. I disagreed with many of his points,
and honestly, the test essentially backfired because I felt like *he* wasn't
mature or worldly enough to discuss perspectives different than his.

I remember constantly going back to my Kamran mantra – "at
least he's cute." I recalled many first dates with the men of Grindr,
even less "worldly" or baseline "intelligent" than Kamran that went
much better, and where I felt a stronger connection. At the end of
the day, I was a dating snob in some respects, but as long as I had
enough in common with someone (and I have interests ranging from
Love and Hip Hop to classical music), I valued that much more than a
person's worldviews on generic and global topics. My life at school
was already a smartass debate – I didn't need to bring it home with
me.

Our relationship remained somewhat undefined during this time.
We agreed to just go with the flow. We weren't boyfriends, but we
were dating frequently and figuring things out. There was definitely a
certain level of comfort and convenience for both of us, in that we
had similar schedules, went to the same school, and lived near each
other. While I told him I was fine with the casual thing – it did
bother me that he didn't think enough of me to commit more. I
wasn't sure if we were monogamous at this time. Although I didn't

have any evidence, I sometimes wondered if I was just the bi to his sexual. A guy to hang out with and have fun with, between the more stressful and demanding endeavor of courting a woman. He was popular so I wouldn't doubt that he was talking to women, if not other men. But, since I had the benefit of the casual designation, I reminded myself that nothing was stopping me from doing the same.

Of course, I am a perfectionist, even when it comes to dating. Hooking up all over the place is one thing, but if I am romantically interested in one person, I put all of my focus on them to reach my desired goal. In this case, I wanted him to be my boyfriend, and it didn't make sense to date around or hookup with others between that. My schedule was tough enough with school.

In My Bed

After one of our study and dinner dates, we ended up back at his apartment pretty late. I think I had been there once before, but I hesitated to go this time since I knew his roommate would be there. If you recall, this is the roommate I had previously rejected on Grindr. I always offered for him to come to my place, as I lived alone and it made things much more comfortable. Of course, in Kamran fashion, he didn't like to inconvenience himself too much. My apartment was a few miles more south than his in downtown, and his place was closer to school, so he never wanted to go out of his way to come to me. Since we were only ever fighting over a few miles, I finally gave in. One way or another, he convinced me that his roommate would be in his room, and we would quickly go to his room and avoid any contact.

We walked into his apartment, and sure enough, his roommate was on the couch in the living room watching TV. I wasn't sure if he remembered me or not, but certainly by now Kamran must have told him about me. They were part of a close knit and gossipy crew at school, so at the very least, I knew his roommate knew we were casually dating. The only confusion was whether or not the roommate remembered me as the guy who had rejected him on Grindr long ago. He said hi to us, and I could just tell by his eyes that he had connected the dots far before this evening. The inevitable awkward exchange had occurred. I rejected you, other gay guy who also goes to my school, and came here to ostensibly hookup with your cute roommate. He quickly went to his room, but not before saying "have fun guys."

A-w-k-w-a-r-d. Those words are etched into my consciousness to this day. As much as I was sure that his roommate had a full 360 view of the situation, I was also confident that Kamran didn't fully comprehend how uncomfortable the situation was for me. He said "ok thanks" to his roommate. I mentally rolled my eyes as hard as I could. In his usual chipper mood, he invited me to his room. Something about his place, beyond the obvious roommate encounter, still made me feel uncomfortable. It felt very barren and unlived in. Like his parents gave him this bed, dresser, and outdated comforter, but didn't think enough to give him a TV. "How do you survive?" I asked. He said there was a TV in the living room.

I immediately realized we were different people. He didn't sleep with a TV, and he was fine with his only access to a TV being in a common area. Clearly he didn't have the same *Real Housewives* at bed needs that I had already established by this point in life. If I can't have the familiar shrill of Vicki Gunvalson or Nene Leakes talking over whoever the new cast member is on any season available for streaming, I simply cannot rest peacefully. I took note of yet another fundamental difference.

This left Kamran and me in his room alone. You can imagine what one is left to do in a room with a cute guy without a television. We hooked up. Even though I still felt weird being in the apartment, this aspect of the evening thankfully went well. I credit the couple weeks of confusion and excitement for facilitating that. Despite our differences, we had a physical chemistry that had kept this thing going. I was glad that it was seemingly reciprocated on his end.

Unfortunately, after every hookup comes the inevitable "after hookup" moment. "That was really nice, but what do we do now?" I wondered. It was late – do I stay here now? Did he want me to leave once he got what he needed? I didn't mind, I had TV to catch up on. Of course, neither of us said anything, and we kind of hung out and stayed on our phones for 20 or 30 minutes. This felt like a lifetime, as far as I was concerned. My internal monologue was loudly running through my head, and the silence of the TV-less room was no help. Why did it never seem to fully click with this guy? This should be a moment that connected us even more strongly, and perhaps made up for some of our differences, but it didn't feel like that. Not based on the complete silence I was getting from him.

I asked him if something was wrong, or if it had anything to do with hooking up. He quickly said no, and that he was just tired after a long day. Indeed, past-midnight after what may have been a weird hookup for him is probably not the best time for a "where is this relationship going" talk. Of course, younger me didn't like that state of affairs, and persisted anyway. I didn't like dwelling on things – perhaps because I felt like his indecision was tying me up. In the age of Grindr, there is always a dick around the corner, and he had already locked me down for weeks. Sure, we weren't actually boyfriends and nothing was stopping me from being on Grindr, but I liked him and wanted this to work. Perhaps it was the image of us that I was obsessed with. The really cute guy from school, the innocence of how we met – it was one of the first acts of me being gay that I could stand by and be kind of proud of. But on this night, I just felt like I needed answers. I told him something was obviously wrong, but I would leave for tonight if he promised that we would address this tomorrow.

No less than 24 hours later, we were at a "convenient" Starbucks in a rough area of downtown, having our talk. I barely even wanted to be there. Our texting was minimal – basically non-existent – that day. I knew something was up and he was in his head about the hookup. It wasn't even the first time we had hooked up, so I couldn't connect what had gone wrong if previously things went just fine and we continued to date. Something about this one seemed off. He started with the usual blurb, "I've been really busy with school and even though it's really fun hanging out with you…" I quickly wondered, is this fool trying to break up with me? We weren't even boyfriends – how do you break-up with someone you have no actual commitment to. "Look," I said – this whole thing was an experiment for us. We are not official, we are dating, getting to know each other, and (supposedly) having fun. I realize we have some incompatibilities – but a lot of this is better than anyone I have been with before. He agreed. "So what about last night changed things?" I asked. What I quickly pieced together is that nothing about last night actually went wrong. The reason he was freaking out was that *nothing had gone wrong yet.*

As I mentioned before, he was very into "tests." From the forced hand holding in Starbucks on that first date, to testing how smart or worldly I was. What I pieced together in that moment was that Kamran was not actually testing me to figure out if I was good enough for him. He was testing me in a desperate attempt to find a reason I wasn't good enough for him, so he could have a clean break from this potential relationship, which had seemingly gone too far for him. I know he had dated women long-term, but he had never been with a guy for too long. It seemed like even though he was comfortable testing *me* to see how out *I was*, he was falsely more out in his mind than in reality. He was nice and proud and holding hands and making out in public, but when things headed in a more serious direction, he freaked out.

On the other hand, I was more freaked out about those small gestures, but completely comfortable with a serious gay relationship that maintained my privacy (I had one before at this point). He admitted that he did have feelings for me – feelings beyond just hooking up – but it was a bad time and wasn't going to work. "You're backing out because everything is going right," I confirmed. He wasn't willing to admit to that. I knew that was the case, however, since he provided no tangible or negative reason as to why things weren't working other than a time issue – which had always been a problem. Our first date was literally in between law school finals. Perhaps he had started adding up in his head what would happen if things got more serious. Perhaps he would need to incorporate me more into his life, with friends and family that were not so accepting of his bisexuality beyond some phase. Perhaps he realized (with me as an example) that guys can be more than a casual fling or good for sex – they have feelings, hearts, and brains, and might connect with you in ways that a woman never has. He wasn't ready – and that was fine, but his denial about it bothered me.

Can't Be Friends?

Weeks passed by after that seemingly final Starbucks meeting with Kamran. I thought of him frequently, and as with any break-up or even pseudo-break-up, the feelings were fond. I reflected on the good times, and how close I was to having a great thing. A thing that I never even needed Grindr for. It wouldn't help that I would often see him and his friends in passing on campus. I wondered if I just needed to work on him a bit more. If he reached a mental boundary with me that he hadn't crossed before, and if we could move beyond it. I knew that if I set my mind to something, I could figure it out, but was it worth the effort? This all evoked the age old relationship questions – "did we end it too soon," "when is my breaking point" and "did I try as hard as I could?" I knew these sexuality issues would be recurring with him, and were not something I had previously dealt with. Honestly, maybe because the guys I was meeting on Grindr never progressed to the point Kamran and I had gotten to. Sure, only a few weeks in, but by Grindr standards this was a somewhat mature relationship. I weighed my options.

Ultimately, I texted Kamran after those few weeks. I asked him how things were going, but was careful not to say that I missed him or thought about him frequently. He responded with no hesitation, and we began a casual conversation. The texting wasn't super frequent or as exciting before. It never is after your first failure with someone. After several days, I probed him about a possible friendship. I said that even though things didn't work out romantically, I didn't have many gay friends (any, actually), and it would be nice if we could hang out sometimes or study together. It was a no-lose for me; I would get work done and be around someone cute. Sure, he infuriated me at times, but maybe he would be a nice social friend to keep around. He did have redeeming qualities – I admired how outgoing and nice he was, and still wondered how he could be so out and proud despite the wall he hit in our own potential relationship. He said that would be cool, and phase two of Kamran and Lex began.

Phase two of Kamran and Lex obviously had a very different dynamic for us. Kamran had quickly transformed from this mysterious hot classmate to a somewhat nerdy (albeit cute) brother that frequently made poor decisions and often drove me insane. It really could have been a great sitcom, perhaps on Logo. We still studied together a couple times a week, and even went out for food. I realized that even though he seemed popular, a lot of his friendships were on a surface level, and I was likely someone he could talk to and get advice from on a deeper level. At the very least, he was excited to have a gay friend that he didn't need to hookup with – as many of us are in these early years.

Sometimes closeted (or semi-closeted men) only have experiences with other gay men when they are hooking up. App culture has completely amplified this. It gives closeted men unprecedented access to verified gay men near them, but a simple friendship is often the most rare form of interaction. It doesn't help that these apps are full of shirtless bodies. Nonetheless, genuine gay friendships are hard to come by for some of us, and I knew Kamran (and I) appreciated the potential for one.

It was quite often not me initiating these hangouts. He would frequently text and ask me whether or not I wanted to do anything. I would sometimes even turn him down, as I wasn't used to constantly being around someone else (outside of a romantic context) and needed my personal time. In sum, I would say we hung out a few times each week, and that was more than I was used to if a hookup wasn't involved. Kamran tapped into friendship mode with me almost *too* quickly.

Very early on he would be on Grindr in my presence. I would think – seriously? We literally *just* stopped hooking up and began experimenting with a friendship. I don't really want to think about who and what your beefcake are doing (*Love and Hip Hop Atlanta*, anyone?). Nonetheless, I tried to be a good sport. With time, I continued to solidify that Kamran and I would not work out personality-wise for a relationship, despite our physical chemistry. I was also back on Grindr myself quite quickly after Kamran. Sure, I was a bit more tasteful than him in not showing him the dick pics I received for mutual consideration, but "perhaps this is what gay friends do," I thought. Honestly, do they (you can e-mail me the answer)? I personally know women do! The girls are talkin', after all (*TLC*, anyone?).

I would try to give Kamran solid advice about the guys he was talking to. The elephant in the room, of course, being that we both knew he wasn't ready for a serious relationship anyway. I told him to be sure he was making clear to guys that he didn't have "time" (in his words) for a serious relationship and was perhaps better suited to a consistent friend with benefits. Of course, by "time," I meant, "isn't fully comfortable taking it to the next level with a man." But as a good friend, I didn't rub that in his face. We all have a process with our sexuality, and we are entitled to one. It just gets tricky when people are unclear about their process with the people they are dating, potentially misleading them. At any rate, Kamran managed to keep these Grindr advice sessions limited, and our friendship continued to progress.

Can't Remember to Forget You

On one of our Koreatown coffee shop study dates, things took an unexpected turn. Once again, he wanted to have a Grindr discussion. I rolled my eyes, wondering why it was so hard to escape this stage of our friendship. Nonetheless, he started talking about a guy – a guy who was *different*. Again, I rolled my eyes. "Ok," I said, "you finally met someone that isn't a complete creeper or loser, congratulations." "No," he insisted, "something is really different about this guy." Why is he telling this to me? I wondered. Again, we were no more than a month out from our own personal pseudo-dating experience.

I guess I was *really* convincing when I told him I was completely fine with that outcome and wanted to be his friend. I guess he didn't have the sensitivity to realize that no one would so quickly be ok with such an outcome. I'm sure it was easy for him because getting rid of me romantically was a relief, and having me as a friend was a new benefit he didn't quite have before. He leveled up, and all I got was a cute but insufferable study buddy. "This guy gets me," he continued, "we have deep talks…he's successful." Things started making sense, after all, even I could relate to the charm of dating a like-minded professional. I had the same "dating a soon-to-be-lawyer" lust for Kamran not too long ago.

He continued with his praise – he's really cool, he lives downtown, we text a lot. I started to get jealous. What hot, down to earth, and responsive professional was Kamran able to pull that hasn't come across my desk? Downtown is my Grindr beat. I know my supply, I know these dicks. I asked him to show me a picture of the guy, knowing that it would only make me even more jealous. Kamran was cute, and I wouldn't put landing this (still) fictional hot guy past him. He became reluctant. "Maybe next time, it's still new so I want to respect his privacy." Bullshit – I thought. Were you respecting the privacy of the last seven guys when you showed me their nudes in every angle? I guess it's fun when you don't take them seriously or want to talk shit about them, but when you find a potential catch you keep to yourself? I insisted – that's not how gay friends do this Grindr advice thing. You have to show me his picture.

"Well, I have to tell you something," he cautioned. "What – just show me the damn picture," I responded. He remained reluctant. He explained that this guy wasn't his usual type. I wondered what he meant. He was being careful with his words, but couldn't actually think of the words to use. What is the issue, I thought? Just show me the picture – I'm not some shallow asshole. I would actually think highly of Kamran if he broke his typical fuck boy Grindr parameters. "What's the big deal," I said. He doesn't have abs? No one does outside of the single moment they are taking that *one* picture they have where the lighting actually captured a few abs. We continued back and forth until he finally flipped the orange glow of his phone into my face. There was a couple second delay before I registered what he was now showing me. My heart dropped – I had seen a ghost. Who was this dick of Christmas past? None other than William.

Yes, William. Of totally catfished me, extremely wealthy, took a photo of me with a telegraphic paparazzi lens on my rooftop pool a mile away, made me consistently uncomfortable, and left off texting me death threats in part one of *The Grid* fame. *That* William. I was in complete shock, and became extremely silent trying to find my words. "What, is he that bad?" Kamran asked. "I admit it – he's not cute and he's not my usual type but he's been nice to talk to and I like him." I began to find some words, and I realized I was not about to hold back. "I know this guy," I said. "What the fuck? Seriously?" he asked. I said it was a long time ago – probably around two years ago at this point. I met him on Grindr, downtown, in the middle of the night – just like you. He was very responsive and charming, I remember. Kamran intently listened – the orange glow of his phone now laid on the table like some crystal ball, and me the psychic.

I tried to figure out exactly how much Kamran knew about William. My senses told me that he knew quite a bit, and he was perhaps interested in William for impure reasons. I started asking questions – what do you know about him? His family? He was carefully answering, and it became clear that he knew exactly who William was (and accordingly, how rich and powerful he was). I reasoned that William must be a lot more forthcoming these days with his identity – perhaps leading off with it as a strength rather than catfishing. Or, more likely, when he's dealing with a guy who is his type – apparently younger, handsome, and intelligent men, he put an honest foot forward.

In the past I had concluded that William was probably being used by all of these younger party boys for his lifestyle, money, and potential connections. But wasn't he equally using guys like Kamran – pretty boys who seemingly have their shit together – to legitimize his own lifestyle? It was one thing for William to land a random party boy – that was easy and probably adhered to the stereotypes his family placed on being gay. But he clearly had his eyes on these soon to be professionals, maybe in his own attempt to bring someone home up to his family's standards. For me, and potentially Kamran, it made the whole situation seem a lot more equitable. The whole "I'm not fully attracted to you, but you need me as much as I need you," thing made one feel less guilt.

It only took a few minutes of questioning before I came out and said it – "you don't like William, you like his money." Kamran acted shocked – but not shocked enough, if you know what I mean. He relied on his prior set-up of the situation, "no, I told you he's not my usual type but it's really nice to talk to him." "Ok, whatever helps you sleep at night," I replied. I pointed out examples of the last several men he had shown me on Grindr as guys he would consider hooking up with – all typical hot LA gays. I questioned how his taste could have suddenly expanded overnight. Again, he relied on personality. He said the typical guys were impossible to have a conversation with – they didn't think beyond their own vanity. Granted, that was a valid point.

I sat there in my thoughts for a while. On the one hand, I was thinking *who is* Kamran to call other guys vain, he's basically the same as all of them but in school, does that make him superior? It seems like all it takes to brand yourself as superior to the sea of gays is to have any amount of self-awareness. "I'm not like them because…" As long as you are capable of making that statement and differentiation, you could set yourself apart and make wholesale judgments of others. I wondered, was I any different than Kamran? Surely I made similar mental judgments about how hard it was to find a guy with substance. I questioned whether it was fair of us to come to those conclusions at all. We're on an app that is primarily designed for hookups; it's hardly fair to make judgments on depth when people are in an "actively seeking sex" state of mind. It's like taking the SAT hung over – probably not the best time to get graded on your intelligence.

I got out of my head. This wasn't the time for an existential debate of my own intelligence that could potentially land me in Kamran's court. He wasn't that damn nuanced or sophisticated – this was clear-cut. He has a verifiable type, he always pursued that type, William does not resemble that type at all, but William has money. Kamran was no different than me years prior. He was essentially tricking himself into the idea that he had more depth than judging men on looks, but conveniently only did so for a guy with money and power. If you recall, back then I questioned whether or not I pursued William thinking that his successful lifestyle would compensate for the shame I still felt in being gay and presenting that to my family. Well, he's not a girl, but he's notable and successful – and if you can't accept that, well jokes on you because I'm rich now and don't need you. William's money served as an insurance policy for the potential outcome that your family would disown you if you really went through with this gay lifestyle. It's a thought I considered then, and I had no doubt Kamran was considering it now. He wasn't in this for the sex. But I could buy that they had good conversations and were on each other's mental level.

I warned Kamran to be careful. I said something along the lines of — you know, if you're in this for the wrong reasons you are definitely going to hell. I also mentioned to him that if our dynamic of discussing Grindr hookups after our own dating wasn't awkward enough, he just amplified it by 100 in dating someone I had dated in the past. It's like Kamran had a book on how not to be a good gay friend, and was trying me chapter by chapter. We were literally in a hot and heavy dating exploration less than a couple months ago. I told him I probably didn't want to discuss his relationship with William beyond this present conversation and warning — it would be too uncomfortable and I already mostly disagreed with his reasons for pursuing him. He seemingly understood, and went about his new life with William.

I distanced myself a bit from Kamran after this revelation, but kept the lines of communication open. At the end of the day, this was a train wreck waiting to happen. It was like looking into a telescope pointed at my own past, I knew all of the players and all of their issues, and it just wasn't going to work. I remember taking another study session with Kamran in the next couple of weeks purely to figure out what was going on with William. He didn't say anything — it seemed that he was doing something I had asked him to (for once). But disregarding my own prior instruction, and assuming the shit had (or was about to) hit the fan in the span of a couple weeks, I asked Kamran for a William update. He cautiously began talking — are you sure you want to hear about it? I said "yes — more time has passed — it was a long time ago for me — I don't care, I just want to support you." I was lying out of my teeth, I just wanted to rejoice in his failure.

He told me that things were going great. I stared at him, expressionless. He had to be joking. He continued — "I'm really starting to fall for him. I think I'm in love." Are you fucking kidding me, I thought to myself. First of all, how does your non-committal-to-men-ass fall in love with someone in a matter of weeks? Someone who is not your physical type at all? How are you convincing yourself that this is happening? Either you're plain stupid or smarter than I think to mentally trick yourself – but whatever you're doing is not reality. I responded with something like "Wow – really? How does that happen so quickly?" He explained that they just really connect in a way he's never experienced before. Of course, it was impossible not to take that as a shot to my heart, since I earnestly tried to connect with this asshole only a little more than a month ago, and he had some hold-up in taking it to the next level. Perhaps I continued to take so much of this personally because I wasn't ultimately in control of his feelings or the "break up," of sorts. If I had dropped you, I wouldn't care – but you didn't want to continue with *me*.

Nonetheless, I told him to take things slow with William. I again urged him to consider the reasons he's with William. Perhaps the financial security was making the lack of physical connection hazy. To that, Kamran responded, "well sorry for TMI but the sex is great." Spoken like a true mistress, I thought. That's exactly what Anna Nicole Smith was saying about that old guy, I'm positive. I was completely offended and borderline disgusted at Kamran's lack of sensitivity in being so outspoken, so I left the conversation at that. I knew this "check-in" was going to be one of the last times I actually hung out with him, because this was getting to be too much. I still knew Kamran was lying (or in pure denial) about how he felt about William, but I figured the truth would come out eventually and it wasn't really my problem anymore. The whole thing was a bit too twisted for my taste.

<u>Sometimes I Run, Sometimes I Hide</u>

Unfortunately, within a couple days, the issue was brought to my attention again. I received a text from a number with no name. You know how those go – back in these days my heart would skip a beat. "Oh God, who did I ghost last year and why do they still have my number?" "I wonder if I could convince them that I was just figuring my shit out, and now it's completely figured out, and we should give it another shot because we really could have been something and I don't have any other Grindr leads." I unlocked my phone. My heart skipped another beat, but not because it was someone I lusted for. It was none other than William. He must have been texting me from a new number because I figured that he was blocked. That, or I did one of my semi-annual "unblock everyone" initiatives to open myself up to texts from men past who may have had a change of heart and want to beg me to be in their lives. It happens, kind of frequently in the Grindr world.

The texts were direct, and they kept coming. The typing ellipsis wouldn't go away. "I know you've been talking to my guy," they began. Again, I wondered what Kool-Aid these two were drinking to be so completely devoted to each other in a matter of a few weeks. Did either of them realize how high of a Grindr volume they *both* dealt with? You guys are on the app 24/7, how do you not have any doubts about the other? The texts continued. It became immediately apparent that Kamran was taking the things I was saying – spoken in what I thought was the confidence of our newfound friendship – straight back to William. "You're telling my guy I'm ugly, fuck you," my eyes were glued to my phone. "You better stop talking to him, you have no idea what I'll do to you," William continued.

At this point, I was overwhelmed by feelings. I felt sick about my involvement in the whole thing. I felt fear from the way William was speaking to me. I also felt betrayed by Kamran – at the end of the day whether or not I was upset about his relationship with William, I was just trying to give him advice and ultimately protect William from what I knew was going to happen. It's not to say William isn't good looking and can never get a man – but since I had a strong idea that he wasn't Kamran's type, I was trying to get Kamran to keep it real and not use the guy. But here I was, facing William's self-indulgent wrath – because *of course* he thought he deserved a guy like Kamran. In fact, these texts confirmed to me that they had a mutually ignorant bliss that made them precisely worthy of one another.

The texting continued for probably five minutes. I was

responding back, careful to be extremely neutral and not provoke William further. I just kept saying things like "ok" or "not exactly," because God knows how Kamran ultimately spun my thoughts by the time he presented them to William. Despite my approach, William's rage only grew. Soon enough, I received a text along the lines of "you need to watch who you're talking about and watch your back, because I will fucking kill you." My heart sank. Surely that phrase is thrown around every day without much seriousness, but based on his anger and power, I knew it carried a bit of weight. He was rich and very well connected – it could be arranged. I was shocked, because ultimately these messages could be tied back to him. If you recall from the prior book, he had somewhat of a public position. At the very least, the local media would be interested if I showed them these messages tied to his number. I pointed this out to William, but he only got even more upset. I withdrew myself from the conversation, waiting for him to stop. I wanted to block him but knew I would only be wondering if he was continuing to threaten me – so I kept the lines open for my own safety.

I immediately texted Kamran, fuming. "Why the fuck would you tell him what I said?" "Do you realize he's over here cussing me out and threatening to kill me?" Kamran acted shocked at William's reaction – but I couldn't tell if it was real or not. Perhaps William took my comments more calmly in person, and this was the first fit of rage from him that Kamran was exposed to. Perhaps Kamran was just playing stupid. Regardless, what outcome did he expect from this? It was clear that he used my negative comments as a point of bonding for them against a unified enemy. "Wow, the haters think we won't last…" said every ill-suited couple in the history of rebounds and shallow dating.

Either way, I didn't care. I didn't deserve this and ultimately, my intent wasn't malicious against either of them. I was trying to advise Kamran as a friend and ultimately, protect William from another bullshit relationship. This wasn't something I initially sought out; it was brought to my attention and I happened to know the parties involved. William was completely off my radar by this point in my life. I told Kamran to keep his boyfriend in check. "You need to tell him never to text me again – I don't want to be involved in any of this."

Unfortunately, the messages continued for several days. This is where things actually got scary for me. William would continue to text me things to scare me. He would confirm to me exactly where I lived. He would drive by my car at school; take a picture of it, and text it to me. He wanted me to know that *he knew* exactly where I was and what I was doing at all times. Of course, when he texted me a picture of my car it wasn't even my car, it was the other guy at school who drove the same car. For that specific text, I responded – perhaps foolishly – "wrong license plate, genius." I wanted to convey to him that I wasn't threatened, but in actuality, it was all I could think about. I was surprised that several days later, he wasn't letting up in his rage. I constantly looked over my shoulder, I only ever really felt safe in my classroom at school, which had a security guard. I tried not to be on foot much, stopped going to the gym and just stayed at home if possible. I didn't know what I was doing, but I knew someone powerful was actively mad at and monitoring me. I told some close friends about it for protection and sent them the text messages.

Now, some of you might be screaming, "go to the police, Lex!" Believe me, I really wanted to. But I knew that as soon as I pursued any of this formally, it would get much worse, very quickly. William stood to lose everything – not only would he be publicly outed, but his behavior would put him at risk of losing his job and his business connections. I'm not saying that from the perspective of feeling bad for him, but I knew that if I reported him he would have nothing to lose. He'd definitely want to kill me even if what he was presently doing was only an aggressive intimidation campaign.

At this stage, I knew he had to be careful, because I did still have some leverage in bringing this to the police. I checked in with Kamran later that week, who told me he had a conversation with

William. He said that William promised to stop texting me. Of course, I knew Kamran had very little (if any) control over a man like this, but I appreciated any letting up. If, for whatever reason, William was dickmatized by Kamran, please lord let it work to my benefit. Within a couple days, I received one final text from William after his talk with Kamran, "sorry man, I overreacted, not contacting you anymore." The texting, in fact, stopped, but my worrying persisted. Silence was almost as terrifying as active threats, because I had no idea whether or not William had been properly diffused. Maybe he just told Kamran it was over but was actively stalking me, or paying someone else to. I printed out all of the text messages and put them in my filing cabinet. Receipts that remain with me to this day.

It was about a month later when I learned from Kamran that his relationship with William ended. We hadn't talked in between the death threats and this news – I really wanted nothing to do with him. I couldn't say I was shocked, and I became worried that William would blame the demise of their relationship on my comments. I never really pressed much on why it didn't work out – I wanted no involvement. Kamran offered a generic explanation – "we were just looking for different things." Congratulations, I thought to myself, you didn't shallowly continue the relationship for personal gain. Well, not longer than the couple months you already fooled yourself for. Thankfully, I didn't hear from William after this point. But it would probably take more than a year before I didn't actively look over my shoulder and constantly fear that I was being watched or potentially attacked.

Kamran thought that our friendship would suddenly go back to a good place after this, but he was sorely mistaken. Perhaps he needed a good gay friend for consolation, but he had burned that bridge with me long ago. Over the next year, I would talk to him from time to time if I was bored, and I even saw him once or twice to confirm my loathing, but I ultimately considered him a complete joke. In less than the span of a year, Kamran had gone from my unattainable dream to my beautiful nightmare. It was abundantly clear that he wasn't a potential boyfriend *or* friend, and no amount of puppy dog cuteness was going to change that.

[3] WHAT KAMRAN TAUGHT ME

As much as I would like to sit back and say, "Kamran didn't teach me shit," I can reflect back and think of a number of lessons. First – Kamran's bisexuality. I went into this significantly before, but I will reiterate here that it is very important to accept how someone identifies with respect to his or her sexuality. For instance, after my experience with Kamran essentially freaking out that we might turn into a serious relationship, I could have accused him of being "bi for convenience" or in some transitional sexuality stage. He was ok with guys when they were just fun to date and hook up with, but as soon as it got beyond that, he completely freaked out. This "transitional bisexual" concept is a very common accusation and assumption that is totally improper. Think of it this way – did you like people assuming you were gay when you were still identifying as straight? Probably not. For those of you who are bisexual or contemplated bisexuality, did you like someone assuming you were gay when you genuinely felt attracted to both sexes? Probably not.

Sexuality can be fixed for some, but a spectrum for others. On any given day, we all fall along millions of different points on that spectrum. For whatever reason, society likes to dumb this down to a handful of understandable labels – gay, straight, bi, etc. When someone identifies with one of those labels as their personal truth, all you can do is respect it. It is not their burden to explain to you the many intricate and complicated thoughts they have about sexuality in general. Sure, when you are dating and it is fairly serious, that may be a conversation to have, but otherwise, mind your damn business. I had a lot of preconceived notions about dating someone bisexual before and after Kamran, but the one thing I've learned is that everyone is different, and when it comes to dating, it is up to *you* to personally understand the sexuality of who you are dealing with, and whether or not their wants and needs align with yours. I dated one or two other bisexual men in the years after Kamran, and tried to approach them with this outlook. You cannot count someone in or out simply on the basis of an overly simplified label. As a community, we really need to cut out the judgments against bisexuality and embrace it as valid.

Another big moment early on with Kamran was on that initial date at the Starbucks, when he pressured me into holding his hand. If I think back to that night, I can still actually feel some of the anxiety I felt in that moment. It sounds trivial, but PDA can be extremely triggering for gay people. You are often drudging up years of suppression in asking or, in this case, forcing someone to publicly confirm their sexuality to a backdrop of strangers. Often, the backdrop of strangers is why you hid your sexuality for years to begin with. Although I obliged and ultimately held Kamran's hand, what could have been a special moment was tinged in a sort of one-upmanship of who was gayer. I hated the way it happened and my lesson here is to approach these situations carefully.

Hopefully none of you would go as far as Kamran and test your dates in this manner, but even if you were trying out PDA more gently, it is probably worth a quick discussion if you're not absolutely sure your date is comfortable with it. Many are comfortable with certain things but not others. Holding hands in a movie is a lot different than holding hands in the parking lot after the movie, for instance. I agree that it is sad that many of us still need to think in this way, but even today as I write this, I know that the time and place in which I carry out PDA can definitely put me in danger. That is not to say you shouldn't live out loud – and I am inspired by those of you who do because it helps all of us as a whole. But in a world where we still hear about gay couples being targeted on the news, it's important to be conscious. All I suggest is that we be respectful of our partners and aware of our surroundings when it comes to PDA.

Speaking of the "forced hand holding" moment, it connects to another recurring theme with Kamran – the perpetual test. From testing how comfortable I was with my sexuality to the early days of testing how worldly or intelligent I was, Kamran was a fan of this mechanism. To an extent, tests are innate in the dating process. Whether in your early conversations on a first date or maybe even in texts and chats online, we are constantly testing aspects of potential mates. Do they have a good sense of humor, are they a hard worker, do they treat their mother right, are they a good tipper, are they racist? These are all valid things people may want to know, but I think there's a more natural way to approach these questions.

Try peppering in a question or two if it inherently comes up in conversation. If he mentions he went home for the holidays, you can say, "that's nice, are you close to your family?" He may say "yes – absolutely" or "no – I literally hate them." Be prepared for either answer, with comforting statements like "wow, that's nice" or "hey – I understand, families are hard." You don't want the person to feel burned by opening up to your question. For example, it would put his guard up if you said "well – family is really important to me so I hate people who don't have relationships with their parents." Perhaps a dramatic example (or not, some of us really *go in*), but you get it.

At the end of the day, very few people like tests, and using them is a high-pressure dating tactic that can backfire. That's not to say that I haven't gone into many dates with this test mentality, but it's usually when I am completely frustrated and burned on the dating scene, desperate for companionship. Testing others is quite often a side effect of not being in a good dating place. With Kamran, his tests put me on edge, and honestly, on the attack. Suddenly, what was supposed to be a peaceful date became a battle of the minds. The way he obviously asked me things to test me had me swiftly reinstate the guard I was barely able to put down on dates.

My approach became, "Oh you want to test me, meet smartass Lex!" He could have learned everything he needed to know about me in a more natural way, which would have brought us closer rather than create divisiveness early on. I acknowledge that we all have deal breakers we may want to figure out about a person, and testing might seem like an efficient way to get those questions knocked out. Think twice about that tactic – if you lead with those types of questions, you risk putting off people who might be right for you. With some patience and a gentle approach, you can get the answers you need in a fair amount of time without ruining your chances. We all have an agenda when it comes to dating, but patience always serves you well during this process. Despite all of the apps involved, dating is a human dynamic that requires sensitivity and tact.

Moving on. While I thoroughly covered reciprocation in dating, I will speak here about a related issue – clearly defining your needs in dating. I often hear about dating situations that have gone left, and when I understand more about how the relationship came to be, it seems that many people are unclear on defining their needs early on. I get it – it's difficult, sometimes awkward, and potentially off-putting to go into a brand new dating situation with a list of wants and needs, but I am here to say that you *should* do something along those lines. Fine – don't go to your first date and rattle off a list of what you want – a good texter, 2.5 kids, compassion, and good dick. However, there are thoughtful ways to get across what you are generally prepared for and interested in.

If you are looking for something casual, it's important to get that across to the person you're dating. Maybe they're on the same page – great. Maybe they are completely over the casual scene and only want to pursue something serious – good to know. The point is, communication early on is key – and quite frequently doesn't happen. I see a lot of people agreeing to casual relationships out of fear that they would scare the other person away if they demanded something serious early on. Listen – there is absolutely nothing wrong with simply saying "I'm at a place in my life where I only want to pursue potentially serious relationships." It is your right, and if you feel like you're going to scare the other person away with that statement – good – you are saving yourself time from someone who isn't on the same page as you.

On the other hand, there is absolutely nothing wrong with saying "I just got out of something serious, I'm only open to casual dating right now." There is nothing wrong with saying "I'm really busy in other areas of my life – I just want a friend I can hook up with." Again, maybe not a first date conversation, but can be easily conveyed via text after that first date, on date two, etc. Just don't lead people on or avoid a conversation because it will likely backfire later. You cannot go into something without clarity on the wants and needs of both parties. If you choose to do that – and many of us do – you cannot then start complaining about how the person isn't acting right, how they aren't giving you what you need, and how they just want to play games. You can only complain when the person told you that they wanted one thing, but then acted the complete opposite way. You can complain when he said he was ready for a husband but your co-worker found him hoeing on Grindr. Sadly, that happens.

One final point on this – if you do not know what you want at all, please communicate that to the person you're dating. I completely understand not knowing what you want, but still being on apps and in the dating scene to potentially meet friends, hookups, and to "see what happens." You just have to let people know that – if it scares off a few people who want something more, that's only fair, because you aren't prepared to give them what they need. Please do not lead people on by acting like you're prepared for things you're not. If you broke up with your ex yesterday, I definitely need you to say, "I'm only looking for something casual." Shout out to the 5-10 men that have led me on in that situation. You can't have it all – please don't be a greedy queen and consider the feelings of others in these situations.

Next up is a major issue in the dating app scene – respect, and the lack of it. This comes into play less with Kamran, and more with his roommate that I rejected early on in my Grindr days. While I discussed approaches for respectful rejection, I wanted to further discuss the global lack of respect on Grindr. One thing that I acknowledge and have grown to learn over the years is that respect is essential on Grindr. This is not me preaching, this is me recognizing that I have not been as kind as I could have been to many men – and I wish I was wiser to not have used this app so destructively.

That's basically the premise of this whole book – Grindr is a crazy tool that completely changed our community, but unfortunately, it didn't come with a user manual. These experiences have turned into a makeshift user manual for me, that I am hoping to share with others. Since writing my first book on this topic, Grindr has actually acknowledged the whole "kindness problem" on their platform, and even tried to bring awareness to it through new reporting tools, saying they won't stand for things like racism, and adding social media campaigns to that effect. The truth is, however, that not much has significantly changed, and I feel that although Grindr is responsible as a company, this is very much a user-created problem that also requires user-based effort to fix.

By now, many of us have heard phrases like "no fats, no fems, no Asians," describing the very toxic culture arguably bred on apps like Grindr where the epitome of desirability has for some reason become a cisgender, masculine-presenting, white guy with a perfect body. Many books can be written on this topic by professionals far more qualified than myself, but I definitely know a few things through my own efforts to bring awareness to it. Honestly, it's no surprise that this stuff happens on Grindr. Grindr is simply a microcosm of a world, specifically a gay community, which sadly includes a ridiculous amount of body shaming, fem shaming, and racism. When you put that world on a grid in the palm of someone's hand, where he can hide behind a faceless photo and essentially never be traced to what he is saying, his true colors suddenly appear.

The situation is worsened by virtue of the fact that 80-90% of these men are horny when actively using the app, completely dumbing them down to a primal state where they think they are entitled to their end (hooking up) by any means (being a complete asshole). Suddenly, it is ok to have cheeky profile descriptions like "no rice or beans," quite obviously and disgustingly disinviting Hispanic or Asian men from messaging them. Similarly disgusting, it suddenly becomes ok to reduce races to stereotypes – "big dick Black men only." You have men thinking it's ok to say "act like a man – if I wanted a bitch I'd be straight." Then you have men who think they are being respectful by saying things like "be fit and white– sorry, just a preference."

The "preference argument" is immediately tossed around on Grindr by perpetrators of the aforementioned behavior. They feel that you cannot "affirmative action" a dating app. You cannot force them to be attracted to someone Asian if they are genuinely only attracted to white men. You cannot force them to be attracted to a thick man when they only like a muscular man. But, as has been reiterated millions of times, that's not what the kindness movement (aka, being a decent human) is about. No one expects anyone to date, have sex with, or even talk to someone that he isn't attracted to. That's everyone's personal right. But we need to stop thinking of Grindr as some private club, and treat it for what it precisely is – a public forum. If we wouldn't say something in real life, we shouldn't say it online, either.

Sure, Grindr has been designed to put visuals and aesthetics first in a photo-only grid, but that doesn't mean there aren't humans with minds, hearts, and feelings reading every word on the platform and more importantly, between the lines. What do you think happens to a young Black man exploring his sexuality on Grindr when 33 of the 100 men on his local grid include a statement about how he is not allowed to message them? What do you think happens to a young boy with body issues exploring his sexuality on Grindr when 78 out of 100 men on his local grid say he has to be muscular to message them? By the way, I acknowledge that saying "don't say it online if you wouldn't say it in real life" is not a true fix to the core of the problems. Just because a racist doesn't have a racist Grindr profile doesn't mean he isn't still racist. I'm not sure if we can ever fully fix *those* global issues in this lifetime, but I know we can remove them from public forums, and that would be a huge step.

Grindr has created a new gay class system, where suddenly entire populations of men are arbitrarily told that they are not worthy of even having a conversation with others. They are not worthy of their attention or affection. *They are not worthy.* Because this subset of self-attributed elite men is looking for sex, they can do whatever damage they want to pursue it. How is that any different from prejudicial treatment in real life? How is that different than segregation based on physical characteristics? You can go blue in the face trying to explain this to guys defending the "preference argument," because they have never and likely *will never* in the future be discriminated on any of the characteristics they judge others on. They don't get it – they think they're just *one* fit white guy on a dating app looking for sex. But quickly, they add together with thousands of others, and create a culture of judgment and oppression that has done irreversible damage to our community.

How do we fix this? Simply being respectful of the fact that Grindr is a tool used by all types of men to meet all types of men. Your preferences, even if they are not as disgusting as the above examples, do not need to be advertised to the public like a billboard. Use your profile to describe yourself or what you are looking for (as in *what* you are using the app to seek, not the physical attributes of *who* you are using the app to seek.) Show your personality, share a joke, make a statement about how ridiculous the app is. I don't know why some men think they're so damn important that they can have a laundry list of traits they will accept or deny in other humans. Those men are the actual toxic waste of the landfill that is Grindr. Some men have gotten so much attention that they feel that they need to do crowd control – "I know I'm hot, so to save you time, please be white if you want to talk to me." Like what the actual fuck – be kind, humble, and respectful human beings. You getting off on this app is not a cause worthier than every single person on the app feeling a basic level of human respect.

In closing, it's fair to say the Kamran-William saga left me with a lot to think about. I always find it illuminating that someone who I thought was so perfect and unattainable became someone so completely wrong for me in every way. That almost always happens with break ups. I guess when a guy is really cute, it's easy to imagine him having the qualities we want, but that do not actually exist. I did a lot of that with Kamran, and week after week, my image of him kept unraveling. Even when it was over for us romantically, he continued to disappoint me as a friend.

He was a double whammy for gay disappointment, but I guess he had the benefit of that real-life school connection that kept me attached a bit longer than I would have been for more of an online stranger. That's not to say that Grindr wasn't laced throughout our entire relationship. Kamran acknowledging that he knew of and used Grindr quickly set a flirtatious tone for us. The fact that I had previously rejected his roommate on Grindr made things completely awkward. When we ended things, Kamran and I were both immediately back on Grindr. And how can I forget that Grindr is how Kamran met William (a terrifying turn of events in an already dramatic story). I'm left wondering – was my non-Grindr relationship completely sabotaged by Grindr anyway? If neither Kamran nor I knew of Grindr, would we have worked harder at our situation? I have to believe we would. Grindr is so omnipresent that even when you're not using it, it has the potential to color your relationships.

My experiences with Kamran and William exemplify the fact that anything can happen online – and you never know whom you are talking to. Grindr is a scary place, and even if you dodge a bullet (as I thought I had with William) you never know when it can come back to surprise you. All you can do is stay true to yourself, honest with your desires, respectful of others, and as safe as possible because some of these guys will resort to death threats over fleeting dick.

[4] LESSON TWO: MICHAEL

On a quiet evening in Downtown LA I found myself completely lonely and fishing for attention online – a familiar story. It has been about seven years since this particular night. I remember feeling stuck in this period of my twenties. I was right in the middle of school – too late to quit, but nowhere near done – working my job at a law firm, always doing homework. My ideas of recreation were binge watching seasons of *Real Housewives* I had seen several times before, or maybe taking my dog on a longer than usual walk. My one true escape was right on my phone: Grindr.

I would instantly tap into a pool of hundreds of men that was constantly updated with exciting new types I had never seen. Living downtown, there was always a conference or an event that would bring fresh, mature (read: sketchy and potentially cheating on their wives) men to my grid for conversations. It was always nice to connect with someone new and distract myself for hours (and if I was lucky, days) with flirtatious banter and – if things progressed well enough – sexts. I generally shied away from meeting too many guys in person during this period – it was easier to deal with them all online, get the attention I needed, and stay focused on the demands of life. This isn't to say that I wasn't open to meeting someone perfect for me (I always was), but I knew that this wasn't realistic. By now, I was appropriately jaded by the overwhelming lack of substance and games that constituted "the Grindr experience."

On one of these nights, I started messaging a guy who was a couple of years younger than me. Let's call him Michael. I remember distinctly thinking – "his face is flawless." No, that wasn't a silent judgment on his body (I hadn't seen it yet), but he was so classically handsome. I remember being excited because he was tall and had a beautiful smile. I could see a joy about him that was especially attractive to me during this stressful period of life. He wore glasses, which I found charming in these final years before I, myself, found glasses permanently affixed to my face. He had this kind of cute-normal style, not a fuck boy or extremely hip, but also didn't look bad in clothes. He was somewhat effortless. He looked pretty fit, but in a normal way that wasn't obnoxious. He had a "gym two to three days a week," body. He was my people.

We started messaging, and I remember an instant vibe. You guys know what I mean. Sometimes it can be hours, or days, before you really connect with someone via an app. It's so easy for the conversation to be cold and rigid – a back and forth with a literal answer to every question you ask. So often, these online conversations have no wittiness, character, or creativity. So many of them are like job interviews, only worse because job interviews end quickly but these can go on for days. And because someone has a cute picture or endearing profile description, you might be inclined to give them extra time to warm up. Imagine participating in a job interview that lasted for three entire days, because you really thought it had the potential to be a cute job. *A no-no.* Yes, this is my book and I can sneak in Mariah references where I please. At any rate, maybe that's the reason why some newer apps have implemented a "conversation window," where you literally have twenty-four hours to make this thing work before the person disappears. That system is probably for the best.

Anyway – none of this was the case with Michael. We

instantly hit it off, and I particularly remember his sense of humor. Why is that shit so hard to come by? It's like everyone wants to show you their body or penis, but where is the damn personality? Why don't you know what the important things are in life? I need you to know Missy Elliott songs from the *first album*, and deep cut references to *The Fresh Prince of Bel Air*. I need you to know how you felt when Britney Spears came out at the VMA's in that nude body suit. I need you to know a couple of *Mean Girls* quotes. Do you know what 3LW even is? Sorry, those were so specific to the late 80's early 90's growing-up experience. Anyway, Michael had personality. We were both making each other laugh. He spoke my language, and I felt like I could let my guard down a bit with him. Talking to him felt like talking to someone I grew up with; I didn't have to explain my jokes and there weren't awkward silences or misunderstandings. In this online world of complete strangers, Michael instantly felt like a familiar friend and someone I wanted to know more about.

I realized the feeling was mutual when he made it clear that he wanted to meet me that same evening. Yes, I found a Grindr gem. Rather than lead me on for days and weeks, he was ready to hang out immediately. Now, for clarification, there are two types of "immediate" guys. First, you have the completely sketchy guys that will say or do anything to have sex with you as soon as possible. That's the bad kind of immediate (well, depending on what you're looking for – *you do you*). This was not the case with Michael's "immediate." His immediate showed a genuine interest in me as a person, and he was willing to back it up by getting in his car, driving more than 10 minutes, and meeting me at a mutual, public location to connect as human beings.

And honestly, I felt the same. Despite not wanting to meet too many guys during this time, something was special about him. Our conversation was going extremely well, and I wanted to know more about him. I did have some trepidation. Sometimes these instant meetings go horribly wrong. After all, could you possibly be in your right mind if you are willing to drop everything to meet someone on the spot? If this was so damn "right," why wouldn't you want to wait a day and plan something more interesting? Maybe there was a romance to the spontaneity, but it made me nervous. Maybe we were both really lonely and blinded by the gratification and comfort of having the other's sudden attention.

Right Now?

There was no time for rational thinking. Soon enough, we were sitting at a Thai food spot in midtown, at what would forever be known as "that time we got the Thai food." To be clear, this was at the most only five hours after we first started messaging online. He was even cuter in person than he was in the few pictures that I had seen, which were already abundantly cute. I was pleasantly surprised and thought, "holy shit, this might be a thing." This tends to happen to me on dates generally – low expectations followed by the "oh, he's actually bae" realization. We sat down at a table, at the back of the nearly empty restaurant. I hoped that our conversation would keep flowing, because the silence of this restaurant was primed for many awkward date moments.

I could instantly tell that he was nervous. The buffer of the Internet was gone, and we were suddenly face-to-face, holding ourselves up to the standard of the amazing conversation that we'd had for hours immediately before this moment. What was so different? We were the same guys vibing via the orange glows of our phones only a couple of hours ago. Except now we kept stumbling into uncomfortable moments of silence. It felt like one of those doomed dates where you keep making what you think are light, funny jokes, but the person doesn't get any of it, and you find yourself in a nightmare of halting discussion, fake laughter, and at worst, completely unintentional disagreements. That kind of stuff kept happening.

I just wanted him to relax and be who he was online – I was

determined to make it work. In general, he seemed kind of shy, but I didn't mind doing the heavy lifting of conversation since we had already established a connection in my mind. There is nothing unusual about being shy on a first date, so I try to reserve judgment and held on to hope that we would get over the awkward hurdle. Slowly, he warmed up. We started talking about the basics, although we had covered most of this already in our earlier conversation online.

He was working as an accountant, but still studying to earn his CPA. I both admired and related to the struggle of working in a field while studying to be even more of a boss within that field. He had his own apartment and paid for his own car – again, something that was not only rare, but also relatable and attractive for me to hear. It seemed that he was pretty close to his family, particularly his sister, who had younger kids who he often looked after. I found that to be extremely sweet.

In LA, that's something that you don't hear about often. Perhaps because so many people didn't actually grow up or have family here, but it's rare to hear about young gay men spending a substantial amount of time with their families. That's not to exclude the reality that many young gay men are estranged from their families by no fault of their own. Nonetheless, it was important to me that he believed in the idea of family and, apparently, was good with kids. I saw myself with kids one day, and infrequently made Grindr connections with guys who I saw as potential dads. We were in our early 20's at the time, so this wasn't at the top of my list, but it was a nice bonus.

Overall, the fact that Michael seemed to have his shit together really worked in his favor and attracted me to him. He was younger, but we were basically on the same page. As the conversation progressed, I began to understand that his upbringing was more challenging than mine. He didn't grow up in the best part of town, and his dad was never around. He told me that his mom and siblings – all sisters – knew about his sexuality, but they didn't talk about it. I was pleasantly surprised that at least he had come out to them – their reactions were outside of his control. Irregardless, I understood. Yes, I know that irregardless isn't a real word, but it was time for another Mariah reference. She continues to use that word, and I would like to support her by memorializing it in eternal print. My book, my rules.

Anyway, by this point, I was out to friends and family, and felt most comfortable with guys in the same position. However, I hadn't really talked to my family about being out after that *initial* coming out. This seems to be a running theme with countless gay men I have spoken to. Interestingly, the dramatic initial coming out is something that they all overcame, but then they find that it becomes awkward to ever bring it up again. Of course, many of them may have been scarred from reactions to their initial coming out, but not always.

I often spoke to guys whose coming out was accepted positively or neutrally, but they still felt uncomfortable actively being gay to their family. It is definitely a process, and it could be difficult to train parents, for instance, to re-hear the reality of having a gay child. Suddenly, you're not talking about "marrying a nice girl, someday." Suddenly you have to start saying – "well, one day, when I find the right man." It's definitely easier to just avoid the topic altogether. They accept you; you keep them in your life, and just talk about everything other than sexuality.

Of course, that only lasts so long before either you or your parents feel like there is a missing piece that you are glossing over. It suddenly feels like you are closeted all over again – what was the point of coming out if you can't actually be out? It becomes frustrating to parents, too. I promise, they didn't forget the part where you came out – but without updates or further conversations, they have no idea what is going on with you and a huge part of your life – dating, possibly finding a life partner, having kids, etc.

My advice here is to keep the dialogue going. It is going to be uncomfortable, and it is going to take some getting used to, but the

worst part is already over. After the handful of awkward
conversations, it becomes more normal for everyone. Maybe after
you introduce your family to a significant other, it can be more
comfortable for them to just ask "how things are with Adam," then
"what type of man do you want to marry?" Yes, it's sad that these
conversations need to be so difficult or uncomfortable, but that's just
the reality and burden of our particular generation – normalizing how
to have gay kids.

I digress, but only to explain that this was nothing I was
holding against Michael. Unfortunately, I did run into a bigger
problem with him midway into our Thai food date. The couple years
of age difference between us was much more striking in person,
mostly because he continued to be nervous. Typically, I liked to date
older or at least my age, but since our conversation went so well
online, I had forgotten about this concern. In real life, though, it
suddenly felt weird. Not because he wasn't smart or mature – but
perhaps just slightly less experienced with a formal sit-down date
than me by this point. After five or 45 of these things, they become
nothing.

I was almost never nervous for an actual date, and navigated
them pretty adeptly. Sure, I may have felt nervous about things like
compatibility or hoping that they looked like their damn picture, but
sitting and doing the small talk thing was easy for me. I don't think
Michael felt that same comfort. His lack of confidence became
somewhat of a turnoff to me. I was trying, and I wish I'd had more
foresight and patience, because he was trying his best, too. But
suddenly, I got a bit colder. I hit a point where I got tired of doing
the heavy conversational lifting. I let awkward silences sit longer,
testing whether or not he would come up with something to say. But
too many times, they just stayed awkward, or what he *did* say wasn't
interesting or didn't flow in the way that our conversation online had.

Perhaps it was a self-fulfilling prophecy on thinking that day-
of first dates never work out. Regardless, my fears were starting to
come true. Maybe the best of our conversation had already

happened online and there was nothing left to discuss. This is always a very real concern for conversations that get hot and heavy too quickly. You become immediately enthralled with one another and leave no questions on the table. Of course, there is *always* something to talk about. Ask married couples, it's not like the marriage suddenly ends when they run out of things to say.

With the right person, there are always more and different things to discuss, rehash, or reflect on. With the right type of person, silence is not awkward. But in these early dating scenarios, we put a lot of pressure on things like conversation and vibe. That is precisely what I was doing with Michael. It was entirely too soon to know whether or not we had an enduring connection, but I was calling it quits on a first date (after an amazing online conversation) simply because he was nervous and we both felt awkward. Looking back, despite how mature and experienced I felt on this date, I now see that it was immature of me to not have had more patience for someone I already liked so much.

I can tell that *he* could tell I that was over the date. I ran out of energy and it triggered a downward conversational spiral. The poor thing – I knew that he was trying so hard and was probably nervous to be out with an older guy who was slightly further along in his accomplishments. Later on, I learned that Michael always seemed to have some preconceived notions about my lifestyle. For one, I think the whole law student thing threw him off or intimidated him a bit. When I think about all of the losers that make it through law school and become lawyers, I can't imagine why – but I get it.

I guess I relate in that I have a minor "doctor complex," for instance. I've been on a few dates with them and there's always that initial "*Whoa*, you're a doctor" moment. But then I think about it and realize that these are just smart people who have been in school forever and honestly don't even realize the way that they come across. They're just people, in a lot of debt, making time for a date and trying to find a life partner in between classes, residency, or practice. Not too different from most of us, really.

I can think of other lifestyle factors, too. I drove a nice car – far too nice for my age at this time. I lived in a nice apartment downtown. To me, all of these things had explanations. I was spending a majority of my paycheck on my car and really had no one else to take care of or spend money on. I was receiving money from student loans to help me live, which helped pay for a nicer than normal apartment. If only I could tell Michael (then) that I am still paying for these lifestyle choices plus extraordinary interest as I write this book. I said it throughout the first book and will reiterate here: it's easy to flex in LA. Everyone is debt-rich.

Based on some of these factors, Michael created a fictional distance between us in his mind. The core of our distance was merely that he was a bit younger than me. At the end of the day, neither of us came from some rich family. We were both working and paying bills and trying to better our situations through education. I was just working the system differently (more stupidly, in fact) to have a fancier lifestyle. But once this distance was etched into Michael's mind, I would fight these notions the entire time that I knew him. I became known as "bougie Lex."

Unfortunately, the date between Michael and "bougie Lex" didn't last much longer. Things got so quiet that I had no choice but the end the suffering for both of us. Even Audrina could only stare at cute guys blankly for so long before production on *The Hills* got the shots they needed. There comes a point in every LA date when you just want to get back in your luxury car, re-apply your mascara, and text your backup man to negate the wasted hour of your youthful beauty. We left the restaurant and hugged on the sidewalk. I remember it being a nice, substantial hug. I hadn't been hugged like that in a long time. Perhaps he was trying to salvage a bit of the distance he created with the awkward latter half of the date. Hugs are a good way to do that – no words involved. I walked back to my fancier than necessary car – an Audi S5 for any readers clamoring for detail – and felt kind of shitty.

I Get Lonely

I slid into my seat, right there in one of those hard to find spots on Olympic Boulevard, and sat for a few minutes as cars blew by me. I felt like I lost a great connection, and I knew that I could have worked harder. Maybe I was too tired for this date. Why did I agree to do it so soon? I knew the risks. Maybe this would have gone entirely differently if I had just waited a few days and met him with renewed energy. Maybe we needed some more anticipation to drive our conversation when we finally met. I felt kind of dirty, in a way. That was the world of Grindr, after all. You get what you want, in any way you want, as soon as you want it.

Most of the time you feel like crap as soon as you get what you thought you wanted. It's kind of like fishing with dynamite. Sure, this was a Thai food date, not an orgy, but the power of Grindr is what fueled its immediacy. Both Michael and I had a mutual knowledge of how badly the other guys on the app sucked, which is why we had such a laser focus on our rare connection. Grindr – the way that it was set up and the types of interaction that it encourages – was responsible for making us believe that a connection of this kind was not going to happen again anytime soon. Grindr made us meet tonight, and I blamed Grindr for ruining what could have been a great date.

Perhaps "ruin" is a drastic word, but in my mind, our chances for a romantic or dating connection were ruined. I didn't hate Michael; I still had fond feelings for him. They were just different. His lack of confidence killed the romance. I had mentally "friend-zoned" him. Of course, after that much talking prior to the date, it would be weird and dramatic to completely cut it off. That would probably have made Michael feel worse. So, for better or worse, we actually continued texting that evening. When he asked me how I thought the date went, I was careful and vague. Of course, it was also late by now so I was cautious not to get too deep and say words that I couldn't take back.

I told him that he was nice, a little different than I expected, but a cool guy. Looking back, I was intentionally not telling him the complete truth perhaps to protect his ego, but also, to keep the conversation going. My problem from earlier in the day – loneliness – had not gone away, and Michael would be a great person to continue talking to. Ultimately, at this stage in dating, I just wanted someone cute to text throughout my long and lonely days. It would have been nice to find someone I also had an amazing, potentially romantic connection with, but I knew that this was unlikely with Michael. I figured at least I could have a cute friend who I occasionally flirted with. I wanted my pad thai, and to eat it too.

I don't know if Michael would have even wanted to hear the complete truth after this date. He was a smart guy. I'm sure that he knew that the night didn't go well, but he was open to continuing the conversation. Perhaps he thought that he could turn it around, and honestly, I was open to it but had only a 1-5% hope that it would actually happen. I don't think that he realized how far the scales had tipped at this point, and I'm not sure why they did. I guess this younger, less patient, and cockier version of myself had a low tolerance for awkward encounters. This was a destructive and counter-intuitive attitude, because I was still cognizant of how rare an intellectual connection like the one I found with Michael was. Why couldn't I have been a bit more patient? Did awkward moments have to be a kiss of death?

Why couldn't I tap into the part of me that saw a man as an accessory? Who cares if he can hold a conversation, as long as he's handsome, dresses well, can take care of himself, is good in bed, and agrees with everything I say and do. It sounds like I was looking for a model with a lucrative contract that didn't speak English and needed me for immigration purposes. With Michael, I was mature enough to know that I should have been patient, but too immature to actually be patient. Whether right or wrong, after the date Michael and I had a new dynamic in which he constantly pitched to me how strong our connection was and why a relationship could work.

Maybe this setup was good enough for him, but I felt guilty. We were both very attracted to one another – that never changed. Another possibility was that I was just hyper-analyzing the intellectual connection. Regardless, it was nice to have someone to talk to who felt like a friend.

In the coming weeks, we continued along those lines. We texted, all. the. time. From mornings at work to very late at night. It was kind of surprising that we had the same strange schedule, or maybe he was just staying up way too late to talk to me for as long as I was responding to him. It was the whole "scales tipping," thing. I felt bad because I knew that he really liked me and he was going above and beyond to accommodate my need for attention. I knew that he was enjoying it too, but I felt guilty that he thought these conversations might be rectifying our unsuccessful initial date. Nonetheless, we continued. I still had Grindr at the time, and he did too. We weren't naïve to that, and it was very easy to see how often either of us was online. I figured, we're not committed nor trying to date, so why can't I leave the door open to guys who might be more compatible with me.

But this did get weird after a while. When you're texting someone about how cute they are and go on Grindr to see them online, potentially messaging ten other guys the same sentiment, you wonder how sincere or special these compliments really are. But then you question *yourself*. Was I going on Grindr just to check on whether or not *he's* on Grindr, or was I going on for some supplementary attention myself? Not only did I want Michael's attention, but I also wanted the attention of others, and would additionally be jealous if *he* was giving his own attention to more guys than just me. Oh the entitled gay webs we weave.

A little more on this universally awkward situation that any Grindr user is familiar with. You met on the app, so of course you both have the app. Perhaps you went on one or two dates, or started texting. It's going well but you are nowhere near any stage of commitment. In fact, it would be quite awkward to say after a first date "ok – I like you so I'm deleting Grindr now to completely focus on you." Surely, that would scare away even the right type of guy who wants to ease into things. So, instead, you do nothing. You both keep your Grindr accounts. The problem is, Grindr is habitual. If you have used it for any amount of time, you are accustomed to clicking into it at various points in your day. When you first wake up, after you get to work, lunchtime, before bed, etc. Just because you met a great guy doesn't mean that these habits disappear overnight.

In fact, sometimes (after meeting a great guy), I would try to use Grindr less but accidentally click it out of habit, not even wanting to open the app. As you know, that one accidental click will trigger your "online now" status for at least 20 or so minutes. Just enough to show your potential mate (when he logs into Grindr) that "Lex was online today." And that is the phrase of death for your potential new relationship. When you go online to see that the guy you've met in real life and are interested in is (or has) been online, your mind starts running. Is he looking for something different? Was I not cute or interesting enough? Does he like me for dating but want someone else for sex immediately? "Why am I not enough?" is the running theme of these worries.

It's a tricky and ironic dynamic. The very means that brought you together – Grindr – immediately becomes the force working to tear you apart. Perhaps one way around this is to introduce a setting (and maybe it already exists) to hide your online status to avoid these awkward revelations. Another option is blocking people once you have met them in real life, but this takes some explanation so that the person doesn't think you actually hate them and ghosted. Blocking eliminates the person from your grid, and transfers them to a real life connection. Someone you have to text, call, and meet in person to develop a further relationship with. I think that this is a clean way to do things, but again, it requires a conversation, which can be sensitive based on its timing. You run into the same issue if after one good date, you tell a guy that you are going to block him on Grindr because you want to focus on him in real life. He might think that you're moving too fast and freak out. He also may be concerned as to why you're so obsessed with Grindr and Grindr statuses. Do you have an addiction to the app? Of course, the answer is *we all do.*

Perhaps the best situation is to let the awkward Grindr "online now" statuses continue until after two or three dates, when you can have a more rational discussion about not wanting to see when the other is actively using Grindr. An additional, and perhaps best option is to delete Grindr or deactivate it once you have a potential connection. Every time you feel a compulsion to use Grindr, just text the guy you're interested in. You might be texting him a lot, but if he actually wants a strong connection with you, it should be welcomed and not off-putting.

Surely this problem occurs on other apps, but options like Tinder (and others) are much less obsessive with the whole "online now" thing, circumventing this issue. The success of Grindr was built on the rush of immediate and live contact – and I can't imagine that's an aspect of the app that its creators want to get rid of. But with other apps, if you can't see when someone is online, you don't really think about it. Regardless, there should be a system or at least an eventual conversation about "deleting the app" when meeting anyone in an online forum. Just be careful to do it when it mutually feels right, usually after several dates so that it doesn't come across as creepy, but instead, genuine and sweet.

Michael and I didn't do any of this, of course. Instead, we just lived with our awkward dynamic. Texting at all hours of the day, and scrolling on Grindr whenever we wanted even more attention. It was toxic and gluttonous, but those were the early days of the app. We barely understood the power of what we had, let alone its present or residual impacts. We continued for weeks. But it was only a matter of time until I became more excited about other, new guys I met on Grindr.

On To The Next One

I had no idea if the new guys I was coming across were nearly as compatible with me as Michael, but they were fresh and exciting, so I was focused on their potential. I reasoned that these guys were very cute, and potentially *more* compatible with me than Michael, with whom I now had an awkward friend-zone dynamic. So just like that, I dropped him. It was wrong and unfair, but it was how I operated back in the day. That behavior is really the core of the endless Grindr cycle of obsession with someone more, someone closer, someone different on a constant loop. The allure of the next dick is both intoxicating and addicting.

Eventually, having Michael saved as a favorite on my Grindr feed became too awkward, even for me, so I blocked him. I remember that we had a bit of an argument over this via text. He noticed, of course, and it triggered all of the considerations I discussed before. "Well why are you blocking me? Do you not want me to see that you're online all day?" I remember affirming to him that we had no commitment – we text a lot and went on a single date. That was the official extent of it, although I can only imagine what he had built in his head about our potential, and I couldn't blame him for doing so, since I kept the conversation going for so long. That's not to gloss over the fact that I still liked him too. I just couldn't get over our awkward in-person dynamic, and perhaps I didn't have the patience or desire to work on it when there were so many other options to pass the time with. I wasn't really looking for something serious, after all.

Michael and I went on like this for months. In a way, we were building a significant connection via text, as the other men of Grindr came and went. I'd get excited about new guys, go on dates that wouldn't work out, and in the background, Michael was always there. We were definitively more flirtatious than friends would be, but I insisted that we were nothing more. Speaking of flirtatious, it was interesting to see how easy it was to slip into sexting with someone who presented awkwardly in person.

I guess it's not surprising, though. Digital communication provides a veil of sorts. You don't have to deal with stares or reactions, and awkward silences via text are generally taken at face value as "he just hasn't responded yet." That is, unless someone is typing for way too long and you're just staring at the ellipses. 3 dots, you thinking of a reaction still (Drake, anyone?). But sometimes, when you're waiting for that critical sext, that ellipsis stare is what ends up happening. Nonetheless, things would often get hot and heavy with Michael via text, and that is probably why all of this kept going for so long.

Michael was fulfilling my need for attention – on the friend tip and the fun tip – and he was so comfortable and familiar to talk to. He seemed to be enjoying all of it, but I knew he was hoping it would develop into more. I also knew that the longer this went on, the harder it would be to ever make a clean break. I would try to distance myself, and it would come the easiest when I had one or two other guys on Grindr holding my attention. But as luck (or karma) would have it, none of these side opportunities were working out.

With time, I started spacing out my conversations with Michael. Instead of texting every day, I would start skipping a day and blaming my busy schedule (which was plausible, but not always true). One day turned into two or three, and eventually with some more weeks, things got pretty quiet between us. I figured that he eventually hit a critical point on his end as well, where he needed to look to other guys to get the same amount of attention. He would check on me from time to time, and I would delay my responses, feeling extreme guilt. Ultimately, Michael really saw something different in me, and I felt like I was crushing his hopes. After all, I knew exactly how it went on Grindr. We were dealing with the same shitty guys who, on average, were nowhere near as put together as either of us and most of whom did not want anything serious. This was LA in the early 2010's, people wanted their sex, damnit. Ok – they definitely still do.

Eventually, in response to one of his "check in" texts, I responded with a more thorough proclamation. I really hate putting myself on blast (said the guy writing part 2 of a detailed book about the intricacies of his online dating habits), but I had these proclamations memorized. Paragraph texts, as I would call them, would poetically explain to men what went wrong as maturely as possible. They weren't always honest, but they almost always got the point across and tied up the many loose ends that came with various Grindr interactions. To Michael, I said something along the lines of:

> "Listen – you're an amazing guy, and we have a strong connection, but for whatever reason it felt weird between us in person and I just can't get over it. I don't think we'll ever be a real couple, and even though it's fun to text, I don't want to waste your time or mine. We both need to find someone more compatible."

This was genuinely how I felt, and even though I knew he would take it hard, it felt good to finally be real with him. He fought me a bit about why I thought it didn't work – evidence to the fact that he was definitely not ready to move on, but I remained strong (for the both of us). It wasn't easy, considering most guys on Grindr leave you on read and ghost you into oblivion. Here I was turning down a guy that was earnestly trying to convince me that we were compatible, and explaining how he really liked me and deserved a chance. Who the fuck was I to shut him down? Honestly, I had no problem keeping it going, but the guilt of postponing this conversation and how much worse it would be later made me go through with it. This was it for Michael and me. I even blocked him to resist the temptation of reaching out on a lonely night and restarting the cycle.

<u>This Lex Ain't Loyal</u>

Of course, the Achilles heel of blocking is unblocking. Apple makes it way too easy. I think I was able to last a few good weeks before needing to unblock Michael and reach out. I thought I would be stronger, and perhaps I thought that there would be more promising men on Grindr to distract me, but there weren't. You truly don't know what you have until it's blocked. But I knew this when I cut Michael off. I *knew* from history how rare it would be to vibe on that level with another guy.

I *knew* it would be a long time (if ever) until I built a similar connection with someone else. You can't go from texting someone nonstop for months and jump right into the same level of connection with a stranger. But the longer I went without that level of attention, the weaker I became. I unblocked him, messaged a "how you been," and he responded nearly instantly. I felt an instant rush of comfort and familiarity. Michael was my sure thing – and no matter when I reached out or what the circumstances were, he would be there. There was a beauty to that, even though it was completely unfair and skewed in my favor.

I didn't actually deserve someone like Michael. Why should I deserve such a solid, sure thing, when I was so willing to block him and move on? Why was he so loyal to me? Needless to say, his character made it even more difficult to navigate the situation. Michael was just ready to jump back into conversation, and didn't even make it awkward that we had gone through weeks of not talking. Maybe he didn't know that he was blocked, but he effectively knew I was cutting him out of my life – I was quite literal with my proclamation. We would talk for a few days, in what was effectively my relapse for his attention. But it would only take a few days for me to realize that the feelings of our incompatibility were lingering.

I knew that I would never see him in the fresh light necessary to build something real. At this point, I was seeking someone my age or even older, someone new and exciting and ready for a serious relationship. I viewed Michael as too young, too naïve, and – if this makes sense – *too into me* to be taken seriously. That could have been the primary issue above and beyond the awkward dynamic. There needs to be some give and take for me to be interested, and I just knew he would always do whatever I wanted to try to stay in my corner. Michael and I didn't have the balance necessary for any healthy relationship – you ultimately have to be on the same level. Obviously Michael doing whatever I wanted would not be healthy for him either (even if I were to accept it).

We went through this cycle for many more months. A month off, a week on. Two months off, three weeks back. It wasn't fair that I kept this cycle going, *but who said I was playing fair?* * Kristin Cavalleri voice, sexy glares into the camera* At this point, I was getting what I needed from whatever source necessary to keep me going, because the other areas of my life were exhausting. In a way, Grindr and this nonstop attention from men was how I recharged. It was convenient and always there, and Michael was almost playing the role of a travel charger. When I couldn't plug into the attention I needed, I had him in my pocket for that back up fix. I knew I wasn't alone – Grindr was an ecosystem of men doing exactly what I was doing with Michael, and God knows the damage we all did to each other over the years.

Once or twice I even met Michael for coffee, testing if it would be as awkward as that fatal first date. On these visits, the nostalgia of not seeing each other helped, but it was almost like seeing a good friend. It was strange, because we had two very distinct dynamics. In person, we weren't awkward, but we also weren't flirtatious. It was like we had been friends for years and we could have a perfectly lovely and chill conversation about pretty much anything. Only via text would our relationship morph into a flirtatious dynamic. Perhaps he got his swag over text and online, and didn't know how to translate it into real life conversations. Maybe it was just an issue he had with me, in particular.

Many social media personalities are this way, actually – totally confident and outspoken online, while completely timid in real life. Michael may have been a Grindr variation of that. It was a strange dynamic that we couldn't shake, but the in-person meetings never pushed us into anything more serious. Within a week or two of any of these on and off cycles, I would convince myself that it would never work out and I was wasting his time, again proclaiming to Michael that I needed to move on for good.

Digital Get Down

To catch you up, we are now close to two years after my initial meeting with Michael. Yes, sorry – that came up on us kind of quickly. Those months really add up, and of course I had a pretty big relationship in between where I went completely silent on Michael (see: Chris, *The Grid, Pt. 1*). But, during one of those longer off-again periods with Chris, I distinctly remember a time when Michael and I actually met up at my place. Notably, this was the first time we ever met up at my place or his. Yes – this entire time, we hadn't actually hooked up in person. We only had our digital flirtation as a proxy for what that might be like.

Once Michael arrived at my place that night, I remember it taking at least an hour to get past our mutual awkward feelings. We sat on my couch, did the small talk thing, and had the TV on in the background. The pointed reads of a *Love and Hip Hop* diva would make up for any long lapses in our conversation. Nothing takes the awkward out of a room faster than Joseline Hernandez telling a bitch she looks thrifty. Though we were never officially together, seeing Michael this evening felt very similar to hanging out with a distant ex after years without speaking. There were some feelings we both needed to get over if this were to go remotely well. Nonetheless, he was wholly unchanged. We still had the ability to poke fun at one another, make each other laugh, and it wasn't too long before it felt like old times.

The big question was, were we going to hook up? I knew just by virtue of him being here that I was pretty lonely and open to anything. Typically with Michael, I would try to spare his feelings and distance myself before things got this far. I knew time and time again that I wasn't taking him seriously, so the closer we got, the more guilt I would feel when I inevitably had to cut him off again. But here we were, in my condo, on my couch. I guess it was too late for me to even be pondering this decision. What was I going to do, kick him out? He came a long way just to meet me on my turf. This was typical Michael – whereas every other guy on Grindr would complain if they had to travel more than 5 minutes to get to you. Here, he probably drove an hour and didn't even mention it.

We hooked up that night, and I can only reflect on the disparate intensity from both sides. At this point for me, these things became formulaic. I was fulfilling a need, quite predictably. A song lyric comes to mind – I think it was The Game who once said, "throw a little Drake on, it really shouldn't take long." That's how hookups felt to me at this time, minus the Drake. (Even bothering to play music was typically too much effort for the Grindr scene). Here was the usual script: invite a guy over, watch approximately 1.5 episodes of something stupid on Netflix, one or both of you are making hoeish advances the whole time, somebody finally makes "the move" and next thing you know, you're hooking up.

It's over before it even started and then you deal with the awkward aftermath of him thinking you actually enjoy his company and that you are going to continue to hang out and watch TV. Meanwhile, all you want is to kick him out of your house in a somewhat humane way (or in an ideal world, he would just know that it's time to leave). That's the problem with not being a complete "come in and let's do it" type of person. The foreplay of reality TV really makes guys think it's something more. Ultimately, making a hookup more casual or friendly does help bypass the deep regret that you gave another piece of yourself to an utter stranger.

Even With Michael, I planned to adhere to this formula. Sure, I knew him on a much deeper level than a Grindr stranger, but I guess I didn't know *how* to navigate a hookup with someone that applied to the gray area of more than a one-night stand but not a potential boyfriend. For *him*, I felt like this was a special or at least catalyzing moment. At the very least, it was a culmination of a lot of sexting and unfulfilled desire – years worth of it at this point – that was finally real. It was our classic issue – he was more into it than me. I didn't feel the same intensity or desire, because I wrote Michael off mentally long before this moment. For me, this was a convenient hookup with a familiar guy. Perhaps I was hoping for a friend with benefits outcome, and perhaps he was thinking that this might lead to us dating.

I also felt a lot of confusion about our sexual dynamic. Without getting graphic (which has been hard to do throughout this series, but a bitch is private), I just felt like real life wasn't playing out in the way that all of the sexting had alluded that it might. Just like texting in general, I assume it was just easier for us to fall into a certain dynamic digitally that just did not work in person. Perhaps we were attaching feeling and emotions to digital sentiments that never existed. Those feelings were certainly cleared up after the hookup, which I felt was entirely consistent with all of our in-person interaction to date: awkward. I undoubtedly acted cold and wanted to distance myself from the idea that this occurrence brought us any closer. I didn't kick him out (I'd like to think I'm a bit more sensitive than that), but I made things so awkward that he quickly understood it would be best to leave.

You Ain't My Boyfriend

I immediately felt a rush of guilt. Even though the decision to hook up was mutual, I felt like I used him for my short-term gain, and completely messed with his emotions. Perhaps I'm giving myself too much credit. By now, he should also have known I was a complete flight risk. I'm sure that a part of him was taking this window to explore a connection that had been important to him, but he knew would never actually happen. He left, and we texted a bit, but it felt very uncomfortable. What he experienced that night was not what I experienced, and it was a testament to the fact that we seriously needed to stop doing this.

This time, it seemed to stick. That hookup was the final nail in the coffin of Lex and Michael. Not that it was horrible for either of us; it just clearly embodied the fact that we were vested very differently in our relationship. It drove home our principal issue, and the fact that we had been dealing with this same issue since we first met. It felt like this power imbalance would never change, and maybe this less than ideal hookup gave us the strength that we needed to walk away. Over the next six months or so, I would check in on him via Instagram stalking. Far better than a text, which might reignite emotions, I could just see how he was doing and remind myself of why it wouldn't work. Of course, he never posted much, which frustrated me.

Eventually, on one of these Instagram visits, I saw that he was in a new relationship. The guy was completely unlike me. I honestly thought that Michael could do better (which is pretty shallow for me to say about someone I knew nothing about beyond appearance). I guess I was purely jealous. Imagine how jealous I would be if I saw that he was dating someone I perceived to be *better* than me. I never claimed to be perfect, people. Eventually, my logic kicked in and I resigned myself to the fact that Michael being taken was for the best. It would prevent me from wanting to reach out again, and hopefully he had found a guy who could appreciate all that he had to offer, and fulfill him in ways that I never could.

Some months later, he came across my @theproblemgays page, which I started in the year after our hookup. He sparked up a conversation, and I was genuinely surprised to hear from him. By this time, I had moved on completely from even checking in on him. I had been on a new roller coaster of dating and hookups, and Michael had become a distant memory. He said that he liked my page, and jokingly suggested that our experiences inspired some of the posts. Needless to say, my times with Michael and many other guys inspire tons of my posts (anonymously, of course). I asked how things were going with his boyfriend. He said they were fine, and for whatever reason, I decided to poke at the relationship. I asked whether he was truly happy, and if this was the right guy, or whether he just wanted to be in a relationship.

I knew that they lived together and relied on each other financially to make it work, a situation which always triggers me. If you get into a fight, would you even have the option to leave? Are you genuinely together out of desire, or is some of it out of financial convenience? He kept answering in the negative, suggesting that he actually wanted to be with this guy. I half believed him. Part of me felt that Michael just wanted to get a relationship – *any* relationship – under his belt.

You don't want to be 40 years old starting your first internship, and in the gay world, you don't want to be 30 years old going on dates saying that you've never had a boyfriend. It happens to a lot of us, but to an extent, it may be a turnoff. We learn so much about ourselves in our early relationships, and it helps when you meet someone who already has learned a few lessons. To be clear – that is no disrespect to 30+ year olds who have never had a boyfriend or 40 year olds starting internships (*get it when you're ready to receive it, tbh*). I actually think that it's commendable not to force a relationship just to say you've had one. I honestly don't know which is better – faking one just for experience or avoiding one and being true to yourself. It's hard out here, and I can't blame anyone for either approach.

In Michael's case, I could just tell by talking to him that he wasn't over the moon about this guy. I knew him, and I knew when he was happy. Maybe they were just going through a phase at this time, but he didn't seem completely into it. I think, like many of us, he also feared the alternative to an average relationship – being single and dealing with the Grindr's of the world all over again. Michael and I messaged on Instagram from time to time, but I kept it clearly platonic. I might have dated in high volumes, but I was not interested in interfering in anyone's relationship. If you want to be committed to someone, do it fully. If you don't like commitment, just be single. Sometimes, I felt like the conversation was veering into inappropriate territory, and I probed as to whether or not he had an open relationship to warrant his flirtatious banter with me. I didn't get a clear answer, so again, I drew a line and tried to distance myself from Michael.

Another Round?

It was probably another year before I came across Michael again, of all places, on a dating app. I never felt any ill feelings toward Michael, and assuming he was single again, I connected. As always, it was really nice to fall back into conversation with someone who felt like an old friend. I asked him what happened with his ex – and he explained how it just didn't feel right. I didn't probe too much into it, it was his business, but a part of me felt redemption in having predicted that it wasn't going to work out.

Of course, a vast majority of gay relationships don't ultimately work out so I'm not crediting myself with a *That's-So-Raven*-esque premonition here, the odds were in my favor. By this point, I had moved a couple of times again and changed a few cars, and Michael of course poked fun at how my bougie tendencies could never stick to anything. The irony was, I was actually not living in the best part of town at this point because I was consciously trying to save money. Michael met me when I was in school and debt-rich, and he was now talking to me after Uncle Sam was asking for his student loan money back.

I had changed a lot since that initial meeting, and it was only a couple of weeks before Michael came over to my new place to find out. I don't think that either of us had any expectations for this meeting, and we were simply eager to reconnect with a familiar person. When he arrived, I was happy to see that he had grown up quite a bit too. I'm not sure what it was exactly, but he just seemed more mature. He was as handsome as ever, and part of me of course wondered if the timing was right for something more. Needless to say, we had our flirtatious banter over the couple of weeks before meeting up. I knew that the connection was still there if we wanted it to be, but neither of us knew which lane to take. Part of me still felt the inequity of power – perhaps knowing that if I wanted to take it there, he would go…and I was feeling a little shaky on my personal convictions this particular week.

It wasn't long before we both decided the hookup lane might be worth a shot, so after a couple hours of conversation and connection, we did just that. It was definitely exciting, and even comfortable to feel that intimacy with someone so familiar, after a slew of complete dating failures over the years. The hookup was better than the last time, but still a bit tentative. We had too much history, and it was hard to just forget the past, at least for me. But I knew things were much improved when I asked Michael if he wanted to sleep over. He said he had to leave early for work, but I convinced him that sleeping over would be more convenient for him traffic-wise.

It wasn't long before we slept, and it felt nice having him there. I walked him down to his car early the next morning, parked in my second spot. Something about that was impactful for both of us. We had a moment of – wow – this is how it might be if we were actually dating. You would live here, and this would be your spot, and you would go to work at this time in the morning. For a brief second, it felt like we were an actual couple. But again, I was aware that something didn't feel right. I felt like he was still more into it than me. I got into my head and felt the old feelings rush back. But this time, I realized that I didn't feel the same guilt. We were both adults, we had been through this many times. We continually reflected more fondly on the strength of our connection than the reality of our actual potential as a couple. Just because you really vibe with someone doesn't mean that you need to marry them. We could be great friends, I had no doubt, but when we infused romantic potential into it, it got weird. We both seemingly agreed, more mutually than ever before, that something was off.

Some months later, I had to move out of that apartment and Michael actually helped me load my stuff into a U-Haul, completely on the friend tip. This was despite only very sporadically communicating between our second hookup and my move. The guy was truly selfless and down for me, despite our years of unfair history. We talked here and there after that, although I never told him where I was moving. I found out he got back with his ex shortly after, so I really wanted to create that boundary with him again. Perhaps I was just a rebound for him anyway.

Knowing that things often turned flirtatious when we spoke, I thought it would be best not to speak much, if at all. He didn't like my approach, but I knew it was for the best. Our conversations quickly tapered off and remain where they have been for years now – non-existent. Perhaps I will run into Michael again on Instagram or in life, and I will always think of him as a great friend. Someone who I know can fully relate to the early years of Grindr and all of the drama that they came with. Michael was at his core a really good friend to me, and made some of the lonelier and difficult periods of those years feel much more safe. He is one of the few from Grindr who I have absolutely no issue with, and I know that whomever he ends up with will be a very lucky person.

[5] WHAT MICHAEL TAUGHT ME

It's nice (and pretty rare) to reflect positively on a relationship that started from Grindr, but I am happy that Michael gives me the opportunity to do so. In a sea of drama and grief, the tides of which are propelled by the dick pics of Los Angeles, Michael was truly a lifesaver. He came into my life at a time when I felt hopeless about dating, and often questioned whether or not "the gay lifestyle" was ever going to work for me. Not to imply that it's a choice, but I was starting to feel very alone and feared that I would never really connect with a guy on any level. It takes a lot to hold my attention – and I'm sure many of you can relate. Beyond just physical attraction, which is the easiest part, there has to be mutual interests, maturity, kindness, and a desire for similar long-term goals in life. Michael provided so much of that, and he renewed my belief that there were options out there for me, even on an app that can be as depressing as Grindr can be at times.

Of course, it didn't ultimately work out with Michael, and now it's time to dissect some of the reasons behind that. First and foremost, "that time we got the Thai food." In a very rare (but not unprecedented) occurrence on Grindr, my first respectable date with Michael was literally on the very same day we ever spoke. As I mentioned, this was both exciting and concerning. Very infrequently would I be able to connect with someone as quickly as I did with Michael, so in a lot of ways, it felt completely right to go with the flow and meet immediately. We both had that sudden "what is happening right now," rush, and we wanted to act on it before it potentially dissipated. Looking back, I highly doubt that either of us would just ghost or that the conversation would have fallen flat the next day if we didn't meet, but meeting immediately was a bit of an insurance policy against either outcome.

At the same time, I was concerned about meeting so soon. There was an air of desperation (on both of our parts) for needing to do so. After all, if we had such a strong connection, wouldn't it need to last more than just a day to actually prove itself? I was also worried that meeting in person too soon would kill our conversational momentum. How many more things could we talk about in a day beyond what we had spoken about online? Meeting someone in person comes with a lot of pressure – everything needs to be as expected or better. The physical connection, the mental connection, the conversation. We had already talked for hours and were both admittedly tired, which provided a lot of fuel for things to go poorly.

I will never know whether it was a self-fulfilling prophecy, exhaustion, impatience, immaturity, or simply incompatibility that ultimately made our date so awkward that night. Honestly, it was probably all of the above. All of this begs the question, when is it appropriate to officially meet someone from an app in person? Am I rushing or doing things wrong? Well, to keep it absolutely real, I have no idea and there is no one-size-fits-all answer. But I will try to offer a helpful way to think about it.

For one, meeting on the same day you connect online comes with a lot of risks. Sure, there are scenarios where the spontaneity of a same-day meeting outweighs the risks of it potentially going badly. Perhaps you are on vacation and only in town for a short period of time, or vice versa for someone visiting your area. Here, you might miss out on a rare opportunity to meet a person you're vibing with, so it might make sense to go for it. Also, due to the circumstances, you might have more of a casual vibe that takes the pressure off of the "first date." Maybe you're both just looking for a hookup with slightly more substance than just hopping in bed. Maybe you're using an app to meet friends; maybe you use apps as a buffer for meeting someone in a bar. Hell, you might even be using an app *in a bar* to see if anyone else in the bar is approachable (is that a scene? I'm too old to go out.) Regardless, there are clearly scenarios where meeting someone right away isn't the end of the world.

On the other end of the spectrum are situations similar to Michael and I. You both live in the same city, you are looking to date or are open to a serious relationship, and you have this instant attraction. While I can't preach and tell you *not* to do what I did, I would caution you to try to delay gratification. Even though this person seems amazing and fleeting, if this is something that is genuinely going to last, it will be there tomorrow, the next day, and next week. If one of you is more eager than the other, try to explain this reasoning to bring the other person onto the same page. "This is going so well and I'm really enjoying talking. Let's continue for a few days and see how things go." Sure, it might sound a little cold initially, but it really gives you a chance to experience more angles of the person you're talking to. Rushing in dating provides no material benefit beyond appeasing a self-serving "I want it now" mentality. And if that is actually your mentality, are you going to be prepared for the work and issues that come with a potentially rewarding long-term relationship?

Chatting online can often serve as a microscopic honeymoon period – you are going to ultimately have differences with this person, but they might be hard to come across in the first few hours of amazing conversation. Without being a complete killjoy, there are a lot of benefits to delayed gratification – mostly by giving you time to assess your potential match with your brain, and not just relying on blind, initial excitement. I'm not sure if more time with Michael would have made me think of him differently, but I bet it would have allowed for a date that I would show up to with more patience, energy, and understanding, which may have paved the way for a better outcome for us.

Of course, after that initial date, I think it is completely up to both parties to figure out how often to meet up. Again, I caution against constantly being together too soon (which is often an early instinct). Conflict rarely appears early on and it's exciting to have a new person in your life, so why wouldn't you want to be with them? But based on my experience, a little patience is beneficial. Most of us have been single for a minute. What are a few more days, weeks, or months before officially committing to someone and spending extensive time together? It's always best when things happen organically, which gives you time to more maturely assess your potential compatibility and issues with a person, and whether those work in a way that makes sense for you to be together. Rush into things too soon, and you may be faced with unexpected compatibility issues in the awkward predicament of being in an official, committed relationship. Use your commitment grace period – it makes things a lot less awkward should you need to walk away from the relationship.

Another recurring and perplexing issue with Michael was whether or not we were operating in the friend zone, in pursuit of romance, or some blurred reality in between. The latter is almost certainly the answer, but as with many gay relationships, we were constantly lying to ourselves about the reality of our "status." Initially, with Michael and with most initial Grindr interactions, the default is that there is some sexual or romantic intent. The vast majority of app users are not just seeking to make friends, despite countless men claiming exactly that with a shirtless profile picture and description alluding to their sexual preferences. Of course, there are some men genuinely seeking friendship, and their profiles appropriately match that intent. I totally support those guys, who are often bashed for "seeking the wrong thing in the wrong place." At the end of the day, it is really hard for most of us to meet gay friends

– so I can't blame them for going to the one place where everyone is indeed gay and ready to chat. But back to my point – Grindr interactions are generally intended for relations unbecoming of friendship.

I guess where it got tricky with Michael was after our first meeting, when things became awkward and I was unsure of how I wanted to move forward. It was clear that I really enjoyed his attention and conversation, and didn't want to lose it despite being pretty sure that we wouldn't work out romantically. In short, I was being selfish. Sure, he was enjoying the attention and conversation, too – but if one person knows that things will never work for them in the way the other wishfully perceives, the right thing to do is to cut it off. It may be hard, unpleasant, and work against your interests, but you are saving both sides a lot of future grief. What gets messy is when you're not actually sure if it will *never* work out, or if there is a sliver of hope. That "sliver of hope" line of reasoning has led to buckets of tears and heartbreak for pretty much everyone who has ever dated.

Because we're not actually sure, or we have convinced ourselves that there may be some hope, we string along unhealthy situations. It's kind of like when you're eating your favorite food and your stomach starts to hurt. You know you should stop, but it tastes so damn good and if you wait longer it'll be cold and not the same so you just keep going, hoping it works itself out. Your stomach almost never miraculously feels better. You have to deal with what you ate. And in dating, you have to deal with who you played. *Mm.* Of course, your stomach processes that extra food and you move on. Unfortunately, men have a tendency to linger longer than a few extra lemon pepper wings.

Too many of us operate in a messy gray area when we know, or at least have a strong idea, that what we're doing doesn't feel right. Sometimes we keep it going because we're afraid to lose the person, or because we think there's no one better to replace them (even if they're not a great fit). But that's not fair to the other person. You should pursue relationships because you want to, not out of fear of having nothing or just because the person is good enough for now. I promise Wing Stop will have more lemon pepper wings next week; it's ok not to eat these tonight. Besides, by then you might want to try a new flavor. May I recommend Spicy Korean Q?

This on and off, friends but flirting interaction went through numerous cycles for Michael and I. These cycles came with a lot of guilt, confusion, and disappointment on both sides. I think the one way that you can combat this "friend zone" issue (in this context) is through transparency. So long as you are honest with the person about your feelings, it is up to you two to continue a relationship in the gray area. I tried this with Michael several times. I often told him that I didn't see us with romantic potential, but we continued speaking anyway. While this didn't completely erase my guilt or confusion, it was at least honest. Both of us made a choice about how to proceed. Here, neither of us had the strength to definitively walk away (for a long time), but ultimately, we couldn't blame one another. He knew what I wanted out of our relationship (i.e. attention), and he chose to engage. I do feel that I should have had the strength to walk away, which would have saved him a lot of grief, but that's not what happened. We engage in relationships from all types of emotional places. At this time, I was lonely and needy – so I took what I could get.

That's why it's so important to approach dating from a place where you feel whole. None of us are ever perfect, but if you go into the dating market with damage or desperation, you will probably just end up hurting people. It's important to feel more or less happy, fulfilled, and independent when beginning to seek a relationship. Take time after your breakups to heal. Seek therapy, talk with friends and family. Make sure that you are pursuing your dreams in life and otherwise meeting your potential. Take care of your health – both physically and emotionally. When you go into dating from this "complete" or "tank full" (see: Vicki Gunvalson) type of place, you are much less likely to get hurt, or to hurt others.

You will have a fresh perspective by which you can truly evaluate people with clarity, and genuinely understand whether you are a good fit for one another. Now, none of us can ever be perfect and all of us deserve companionship, so it's never going to be that rosy, but you get the idea. If you have a major issue in life that you need to tend to, dating won't magically make it better. Most often, it will distract you from the problem, the relationship won't work out, and ultimately you will be worse off because the problem has grown while you ignored it.

A related issue that transparency and the friend zone bring up is the idea that things can often be hot and heavy with someone online, and then awkward in person. This was often the case for Michael and I. There is a very simple reason for this: the veil of anonymity provided by digital interaction. Whether on Grindr or text, when you don't have a person in front of your face, it is so easy to avoid all of the real-life nuances that potentially make things awkward.

You assign the qualities you desire to the person you're talking to, and they almost function as a robot behind your imagination, typing responses that you interpret from a false perspective that pleases you. They might as well be a literal chat bot with a picture (hell, some of them are). I think that's actually what's so exciting about Grindr. It's all digital — so you are imagining how a person sounds, looks, feels, and acts. They are typing to you, but you are reading it in a way that satisfies you. That's why first dates or phone calls can be so awkward. This person you thought was your soul mate suddenly has really long pauses before answering you, or laughs at the wrong time, or doesn't understand your sarcasm.

Digital communication shields us from all of that. Of course, that can make things really awkward in person. For Michael and I, things were so easy online. We had a lot in common and similar personalities, so the conversation would always flow. That is half the battle in talking to someone online. The issue was, in person, his level of comfort and confidence was finally brought to the forefront.

There was no more app to hide behind. It was clear many times that he wasn't as confident in approaching me in real life as I interpreted him to be when talking online. For what it's worth, the other stuff was there. He laughed at the right times, understood my sarcasm, etc., which is why I always considered him a great friend.

But, in relationships, intimacy is important – and that's where things never really connected for us. We were attracted to each other, but sometimes chemistry isn't enough to bridge the gap. It's like when someone who you think is the hottest person turns out to be a horrible kisser (not talking about Michael here). Everything you think and imagine about the person suddenly becomes meaningless because you can't connect in the right way. There's not much that you can do to overcome this "awkward in real life" scenario, other than being mindful of it. Don't become so attached to someone online that you become overwhelmed or disappointed by who they are in person. It's happened to me more times than I can count on Grindr. "I can't believe I thought that this horny nerd wearing dad cargo shorts in the year of our lord 2019 was the answer to my solitude," I've said more times than I'm proud of at a Starbucks date stuck with said man. It's always best to keep an open mind, and when you feel comfortable, try to meet a person in real life (in public) before things go too far online. In the early days, I even said "I love you" to guys I hadn't met in real yet, just off of weeks of texting. Brilliant.

Also, to the extent possible, try to be fair and give people chances. This is something I wish I'd had the aptitude and patience to do with Michael. Going from an Internet interaction to real life can be tough and overwhelming for many people – people who might actually be really great for you once you get over the initial hurdles of awkward or unexpected interactions. I can't give you a hard rule to live by, but if you like many aspects of who you were talking to, try to give them two to three dates before giving up on the connection or making a wholesale judgment of incompatibility. Of course, if you barely like them to begin with, and the first date is nothing like you expected, please walk away and save yourself the grief. But given that our modern reality mandates meeting people in such a bizarre digital landscape, we could all stand to be a bit more patient and understanding when we think we might have stumbled upon a solid match.

Moving on. An issue I have spoken about quite a bit online is age differences in dating. With Michael, this would seem to have been a trivial issue (we were not too far apart), but your specific age range can make a complete difference. An 18 year old and a 24 year old, while not several years apart, may be in completely different places in life. One can't order a drink at a restaurant, and the other might be wrapping up grad school. Not to say that the younger guy can't be more mature, *raises hand*.

But, for a labyrinth of reasons, age differences can completely alter the dynamics of a relationship. My being older definitely led to some level of intimidation on Michael's part. Maybe he felt that I was in a different place in life, or that I was interested in different things than he was. This seems strange, as we had so much in common online, but baggage associated with age can do that to relationships. I think about it like this: when you were in 6th grade, didn't the 8th graders seem infinitely cooler than you? They were literally no more than 2 years older than you. Sometimes, people get stuck in their head about ages in that way, but generally, as we get older, we tend to care less about the number and more about the actions and life experiences of the person.

In the past, I've been known to date guys a few years older than me. I generally found that guys my age weren't as mature as I was in my early 20's, and there was something exciting about dating a guy who appeared to have his shit together. By the way, that is a complete generalization because a ton of men older than me (then and now) have absolutely nothing together – but that's a different book. The point is, my perception of guys a few years older biased me to feel that they had something more to offer. I assumed more maturity, more experience, more stability, and perhaps more willingness to settle down. I assigned attributes to an entire of group of men completely based on age (most of whom didn't have the things I perceived).

Ultimately, it boils down to the two people contemplating a relationship. Whether older or younger, you might always be surprised by who you are dealing with. What you thought might be an impediment with a younger or older guy may completely reverse. For example, younger guys might be way more willing to settle down than older guys who might be jaded from years of dating (one of a thousand stereotypical hypotheticals). That said, I do not adhere to the cliché that age is just a number. There are many rules of thumb that generally hold true. Younger guys *do* generally need to discover who they are and what they want to do in life. That's not so hard to believe. Accordingly, they may *think* that they know what they want in a relationship, but just by virtue of being younger, they may still have a lot to learn.

When I was really young, I would hate when people would categorize me in this way. I felt that I knew who I was, exactly what I wanted, and was very mature. Sure, those things were true to me *then*, but my God have I learned a ton in the past decade. That doesn't mean I should not have dated, or that I was lying to the guys of my past about my maturity, but it's just something to keep in mind. We are always learning and growing, and what we *think* we want will continually evolve. This can be a tricky issue in relationships with two young people, which seem so exciting and real, but many times are outgrown by one or both parties in a few years time.

Another rule of thumb is that older men may find themselves single for a number of reasons that they likely know, but may choose not to openly share with others. I'm not generalizing about what those reasons are, because they can be anything. Perhaps a 20-year relationship ended. There can be death or sickness of a partner. They can have high standards and have just not have met their match yet, or they could have spent a number of years focused on their career. None of these things are bad, I am just saying that if you are single, there is a reason, and if you are a bit older, there may be a pattern of reasons that you are more aware of than a younger man. In fact, it would be strange for you not to have a general concept of your dating patterns with age (i.e. I can't commit, or the gay dating scene is complete garbage and it's not my damn fault, etc.). The point is, the more years you date, the more you likely know about what works and what doesn't in your romantic life, and why it is the way it is.

Accordingly, in situations where you may be dating someone with a major age difference, I think communication is especially key. We all mature at different rates, so it's not my place to say that a 50 year old man and a 20 year old man don't have a ton in common; I'm sure that many do. That said, those two people will likely be in very different places emotionally, financially, and as far as their long-term wants and needs go. Accordingly, I think that it is critical for both parties to be transparent about what they want out of a relationship.

Maybe it's just an ongoing hookup, or maybe it is a long-term committed relationship. Either way, given that the stakes are higher with a big age difference, be sure that you are both comfortable with what you will potentially gain (or lose) as a result of this relationship. This requires the older man to be clear about why he feels he is single and what he is looking for, and the younger man to be clear about what he might *not know yet* about what he is looking for. Again, the 50 and 20 year old relationship might necessitate this conversation in a more drastic way than say a 40 and 65 year old, where both parties may "know themselves" and what they want. In any event, age is tricky and although it's not everything, it can affect a partnership in ways that you should be mindful of.

A final, and ubiquitous issue I'd like to discuss in relation to Michael is the potential impact of social media on relationships (no small feat). For Michael and me, this came into play often during our "off" periods, when we had called it quits, knew we shouldn't be talking, but would stalk each other online when we got lonely or curious. I can only imagine how often this happens out there. What I want to say about this is that social media, in general, is another veil of digital society. You never know what you are actually seeing. Most often, people are simply projecting the aspects of their lives that they want people to digest. I want you to think that I go to the gym a lot, so I post gym selfies both of the two times I go every month. I want people to think that I'm well traveled or constantly on vacation, so I have been posting flashback Fridays from my trip to Europe for the past 52 weeks. I want people to think that I'm balling, so I make sure that you see the Range Rover logo from my rental car in an Instagram story lamenting this LA traffic jam.

The list is endless. In past relationships, the people I've dated have hyper-analyzed my behavior on social media to try to interpret who I am as a person. It's sad, because social media is almost exactly conveying who we are *not* as people. For instance, if I liked a bunch of posts of a model, it was interpreted that I only liked "that" type of man (which may not have been the same race, body type, or had the same style as the person I was dating). In reality, these "models" might not have been my type at all – I liked a lot of them because they were fashion pages and I liked the outfits!

I've also been analyzed for how often I post (or don't post). If I posted too much, I was judged for sharing too much of my life online or being a show off. If I posted too little, it was assumed that I was hiding something that I didn't want my partner to know. Then you get into actually being in a relationship, and how often to post (or not post) the person you are with. This all gets tricky. Personally, I don't feel the need to blast every aspect of my relationship online, but I also feel some type of way if I have been dating someone for half a year and they haven't even mentioned me in a story. Are they hiding me, are they comfortable with their sexuality? This, and a million other examples, clearly illustrate why social media complicates relationships.

It can be an extremely treacherous tool, especially in relationships where emotions run high. Sure, when things are going great, social media is almost like a drug. You feel happy and connected to your partner, and you may constantly flash your relationship online to solidify to the world that you have found someone who completes you. Perhaps some of my pettier (no shade) readers might have even done this in the past to rub it in the face of their exes. "Look, I found someone who gives me all of the things that you couldn't, and they're cuter too!" When things are good, social media can be a stamp of approval you give yourself – a big billboard that screams "I'm doing love right." On the other hand, during a break-up, social media can be cutthroat and debilitating. Your ex might be posting pictures with a new interest painfully soon, or you might stalk them to see if they are miserable without you (and it always seems that they are not). You might find yourself passive aggressively posting about why your life is so much better without your ex, just to chop them down.

Whatever the scenario – social media is both good and dangerous, so you should be careful not to draw too many conclusions from it. Social media has almost always led to misunderstandings and sensitive issues in my prior relationships. As trivial as it may seem, it is a huge part of our lives and how we communicate, so it's important to keep it in this context. Not all is as it seems, and not all should be blasted online. The only solution to this social media problem is human-to-human communication. Every assumption and misconception can be resolved much more quickly through conversation than online stalking. It's quite ridiculous that so many of us actually know that much of what we see online isn't real, yet we take it so seriously when it involves our relationships. In general, if you have a secure and mature partner, they will keep social media in context and it shouldn't present too many issues.

Wrapping up on Michael. I don't know if he'll ever read this, but if he does, I thank him for being there for me during those crazy years of Grindr. Even though it never worked out for us, that doesn't cloud my ability to say that he is a great person who deserves only the best. For anyone reading this who feels jaded by dating or apps (and I think that's almost all of us), I hope that you all meet someone as good hearted as Michael to give you hope. Great connections and friendships are out there in the gay community, and the better we treat one another, the more likely we are to sustain those relationships and friendships in our lives. I learned a lot from this one.

[6] LESSON THREE: CHRISTIAN

I was lying in bed, probably around midnight, safely in my bedroom in a shared apartment in DTLA. I had only lived here with my roommate for a few months by now. After wrapping up undergrad in Orange County, I made the migration that seemingly every young person living in the OC wanted to make. The allure of LA, particularly downtown, where everyone was, where everything cool happened, and where things were frantic and exciting. It was a dramatic shift from the manicured backdrop of where I had been for the past four years. Everything was *too* perfect in OC. The only time you saw a cop was if they were pulling over some white guy in a Porsche 911. Everything closed at 10 PM, and literally not a leaf was out of place. As you can imagine, downtown was a bit of an adjustment. There was crime, it was dirty, there were celebrities, and I had no idea where anything was. That said, the frenzy of the new surroundings kept me excited in a way that I longed for.

At this time, my life was pretty much just work, home, and seeing friends. I was taking a gap year from school, and I was finally focused on myself rather than the expectations I had placed on myself of what I wanted to be. By this time, I had overcome but still dealt with some serious depression from my college years, which was layered, but often centered on, "is this what the hell I want to be doing with my life?" I was hoping that the new setting and freedom from my prior environment and expectations would allow me to focus on me. What did I enjoy doing – did I have more of a creative or professional destiny? Nonetheless, I still worked at a law firm to pay the exorbitant rent for 50% of this apartment. That was the only job experience I had, and the firm I worked at in Orange County was kind enough to re-hire me in their LA office. By "kind enough" I mean that I was a bomb worker and they underpaid me at both locations, but it was a solid job for my age. Plus, even though my work was the same as before, at least in was in LA. There was an excitement as soon as I stepped out of the office. The rest of the day was mine, to do *whatever* I wanted in this strange new place.

Most often, if I wasn't seeing a friend, I defaulted to driving around the city and pretending to be cool, or sadly landing right back at home in my room. Work was draining, especially all the overtime I was putting in to pay for the nice things that came with bills that choked me financially. Anyway – let me get on topic. Although I had started exploring my sexuality in college, my options were limited for my age group in OC and certainly in a pre-Grindr world. But moving to LA coincided essentially with Grindr's creation, and many nights I found myself on the app figuring out who was out there that caught my interest. The options were seemingly endless as compared to the Craigslist hunting of yore (see: this book's intro). Every night after work afforded me a fresh orange grid of sketchy shirtless men ready to distract me.

I literally had no idea what I was looking for. Definitely not a relationship, and honestly, most of the guys on there seemed older or way too experienced for the type of guy I would be comfortable meeting. Still, I wouldn't shy away from talking to any of the ones that interested me. I figured I could always block them if things got uncomfortable. It was most exciting to find a guy my age at a similar place with his sexuality – figuring shit out. The other ones were fun to talk to, but I knew if I were ever to meet someone, I would feel most comfortable with a guy similar to myself.

I don't want to gloss over how lonely things felt around this time. Even though I was excited for this new phase of life, I didn't have many friends actually living in LA. I was also a bit of a loner by choice. Sometimes I felt like I was pretending that I moved to New York or something. Seeing friends too often just reminded me of my past, and in a way, I think I finally needed some time to myself to actually explore what I wanted to do with my life – a big part of that was my sexuality. In LA, I didn't really have a fear of running into anyone or needing to hide too much of who I was. Everyone and everything was new. But since I was so picky (and also scared) about meeting with guys at first, I often felt isolated.

The conversations I was having on Grindr were comforting, even if I didn't plan on meeting those guys. I don't know why a periodic message from a headless shirtless man on my phone was comforting, but it was. It gave me someone to message in the morning, in line at Starbucks, or during my lunch break to help pass the time. Grindr made it feel like I was part of something even though I was physically on my own. *Once againnn....one more timeee....*(Patti LaBelle, anyone?)

Thank God I Found You

As I was lying in bed that night, I remember a number of empty Grindr interactions. Me saying hi to no response, or the guy hopping offline right after the conversation started. The only guys who *were* messaging me were ones I had no interest in. But quickly, things changed. It was around midnight when I first interacted with Christian. I didn't know then that it would be about four years of extended on-and-off interaction before Christian would leave the periphery of my life.

As I begin to tell you about this journey with Christian, the last man of *The Grid* series, I find myself reflecting on how tangled of a web these Grindr men were. It probably sounds like I was dealing with all of these men during essentially the same period of time. Genuinely, though, that wasn't the case. What is clear, however, is that it was so easy to accumulate a handful of Grindr "regulars" – a familiar set of men that I would continually run into on the app between serious dating, relationships, or situationships (something in the middle).

Sometimes your regulars would be dating someone seriously and fall off the map. You would think about them from time to time, but leave them alone. Sometimes *you* would be unavailable and closed off to contact from regulars. But given we were all using Grindr, and most Grindr relationships ended fairly quickly, it was more than likely that we would cross paths again. Even after serious and extended relationships, I would inevitably run into a regular, sometimes years after our original meeting. The "Grindr regular" is a somewhat comforting force, if not a bit twisted and unconventional.

But back to Christian. Christian had exciting stats. You know what I'm talking about – and sure, it's shallow, but the point of this book is to put it out there. He was about 5'11" or so, 165 pounds, and had his body type marked off as "toned." At this point in time, I was most excited by guys similar to me in size and stature, but the world of stats on Grindr is both horrible and fascinating.

There were points in time, usually in the earlier days of Grindr exploration, where I was most excited by men with stats *unlike* mine. Older than me, taller than me, bigger than me, more muscular than me (so, in my case, that just meant having *a* muscle). Perhaps those desires aligned with the excitement of wanting an older, stronger, and more experienced man to "show me the ropes," so to speak. And that's not purely sexual – there was just an excitement in the unknown that I know many young guys relate to.

In the world of Grindr, however, these desires are transformed into a visual grid – almost like an Excel spreadsheet – reducing the value of humans to physical traits. It's nothing that doesn't happen in real life, but it's exponentially worsened due to the volume and frequency in which it occurs. For example, you may be at a gay bar and see two guys across the room. You think one is hotter than the other, perhaps because he looks fit or is taller, or is maybe younger than the second guy. You decide to pursue the "hotter" guy, based on your judgment of the guy next to him. Fair enough. Enter, Grindr. You have at a minimum 100 men that you can make wholesale judgments on using data. In fact, for people who subscribe to the premium version of Grindr, the app allows you to filter out men based on any stat. Below 5'9", more than 180 pounds, any race, any age – you can completely eliminate humans from your purview based on self-attributed traits.

Convenient? Perhaps. But what type of damage is this doing to self-esteem throughout our community? How are the men that are constantly excluded based on a number of immutable physical traits supposed to feel about themselves? Why is one man's pursuit of dick important enough to make thousands of men feel worthless in the process? What started out as a convenient way to connect you with the types of men you are most interested in is, in reality, a purposeful erasure of an entire population of gay men.

I digress, but more on stats (and what we can do about it) later. I believe I sent the first message to Christian, who didn't even have a face picture posted. Whatever photo he had – probably some sort of mysterious tank top/gym shorts combo – caught my attention. Christian was a freaking mystery – for a very long time. I basically knew he was my age, 5'11", 165 pounds, toned, and a man. He only sent one-word responses, which is generally not a great way to facilitate a conversation. It was almost like trying to get a stubborn child to engage, but I was quite attracted to him, so I didn't mind the challenge. Even in those messages before he finally sent a face picture I felt like I knew it would end up good. He was so *normal hot*. Is that my type by the way? I keep describing these guys as some variation of "normal hot." What I mean by that is he would be a guy I would see in public and lust after (almost positive that he wasn't gay).

Now, that's a complicated confession. It touches on things

like internalized shame and the glorification of masculinity in society. But for many of us, this is not a novel concept, so I choose to be real and write about it. Our first gay experiences or crushes tend to be on men we fantasize about – men we think we can't have. Many of us seek men that seem as straight and masculine as possible, because it's overwhelming enough to cope with the fact that we might be gay and that the things we want to explore are completely guilt-inducing and wrong. We want someone we perceive as similar to us as possible, to make coping with ourselves as easy as possible. It's almost like exploring your sexuality with a similar friend; it's something easier to brush under the rug. The whole, "I got too drunk and hooked up with my frat bro" fantasy that gay porn so frequently relies on.

But this is exactly what Christian was, and that was why I felt excited to talk to him. He reminded me of myself in a lot of ways. Not to say that I was some model of masculinity, but I wasn't out yet, so I guess I thought I was fooling some people. In a lot of ways though, he was much more of a "typical guy" than me. He was pretty active and liked sports. I would drag myself to the gym, but sports were never my thing and I have always felt like "less of a guy" in life for it. He dressed like a "sports guy" that was also fashion conscious – the backwards Dodgers hat really completed my fantasy. He lived with his parents, which around this age was completely typical. He was really close to his family, and none of them knew he was out. He had what seemed like a pretty good job to me, working for the city in some administrative capacity.

Every aspect of him made him seem so familiar and comfortable. This was a guy that I could open up to and feel comfortable with, despite the fact that he insisted on greeting me with a cold ass "sup" for the entirety of our relationship. We were essentially at the same stage with our sexuality, we had similar values, we both worked 9-to-5's, which was kind of rare for the typical Grindr guy my age. And yet, there was still this mystery to him.

I guess the "opposites attract" aspect of Christian was simply that he fit more of the masculine stereotypes than I did, and I found that to be exciting. There always seemed to be a looming question mark to him, and sometimes I questioned whether he even knew he was truly gay or not. Perhaps he didn't, and perhaps that ongoing challenge of keeping his attention captivated me. Often, when a guy is *too* into me, I lose interest. With Christian, though, he wasn't *too* into anything. This isn't healthy (by the way), but the burden of holding his attention fell upon me – and that burden forced me to overlook a lot of his flaws along the way.

If we were in a mature, balanced relationship, we would both be putting in equal amounts of effort and evaluating our compatibility. In this case, even if I didn't like certain aspects of him, I wouldn't bring it up. That's what happens when you're a part of an uneven relationship. The other person has some silent control over you, and you cannot express yourself fully. I knew that any negativity from my end of the relationship would possibly result in him blocking me and disappearing. This happens a lot on Grindr, and amplifies self-esteem issues for so many guys already struggling to figure out who they are. They suddenly come across this "hot" and "unattainable" guy on the app, and subconsciously (or consciously) give that person complete power over them.

Suddenly, a guy who may not even be using a real picture and whose face you might not even have seen yet completely controls your mood and feelings of self-worth. If he engages with you, you feel happy and on top of the world. If he disappears or ghosts you, you feel miserable or as though you have failed in some way. Needless to say, no man that exists in some fake digital reality should have any control over you whatsoever, which is why you should try to use apps from a "whole" place. By that I mean, you should feel more or less confident and stable about who you are and what you deserve, so you don't get taken advantage of. Of course, that is idealistic and many of us use apps when we are lonely or going through something, which results in the pain I am referring to. Obviously I am guilty of this throughout the stories I have shared in these books, but it is something to keep in mind.

Over time, Christian started to open up to me a bit more. Instead of one-word responses, I would get three or four words back. "Sup" started morphing into "sup man" – an incremental but welcomed gain. It seems that my persistence was breaking him down a bit. I could tell that he probably used Grindr quite a bit, perhaps as an escape from his closeted reality (and same), but was already jaded on the ways guys would interact on the app.

The catfishing, the ghosting – even in the early days of Grindr, it was easy to be over it fairly quickly. Yet, for most of us, it was our only means of interacting with guys in the same position as us – so there we were, bitter and online. Of course, it wasn't too long before I got a face picture, and I found him quite adorable. He totally fit the image of him I had in my head (which rarely happened). He was completely that "guy at the Dodgers game." He was like a straight bro that gives you a double take, and you're left wondering whether it was a "gay look" or a "what are you looking at look."

Reflecting back, it's a bit troubling that my preferred type of guy was a closeted gay man that passed as straight, who reminded me of men who might potentially attack me for staring at them with lust. But I have to believe that a lot of gay men go through this phase. For me, once I started owning and embracing more aspects of my personality that did not conform to masculine stereotypes, I was willing to accept those same traits in a potential partner. At the time, Christian was exactly what I was – repressed – and there was nothing more attractive to me than a guy in the exact same boat.

Say My Name

Within that first week of talking on Grindr, he shared his number with me and we started texting. It seems lame, but I can't even explain how exciting it was to be texting with him. Every time his nameless number would pop up on my phone (because yes, this was a time when we thought sharing legal first names was the equivalent of outing ourselves), my heart would skip a beat. It's like I had overcome this insurmountable barrier and was texting some "straight but questioning" guy. He trusted me, and talked to me throughout the day. The excitement was completely ramped up by the fact that he didn't seem gay. I felt like he was my secret and I was his, and it was such a new phenomenon for me.

Pretty soon, it felt like we were relying on each other to get through our days. My day wouldn't go well if he didn't respond to my "good morning" texts. And I wouldn't feel complete if we didn't check in to complain about work or share what we were eating for lunch. It was basic stuff, but it felt so special that someone in the world, in the same position as me, had made me their "person" that they opened up to. Of course, it helped that we seemed to be quite attracted to one another. I always knew he was my type, but I was slowly figuring out that despite playing hard to get, I was definitely his type too. Just because I was closeted didn't mean I wasn't visually stunning.

Naturally, we moved through the stages of digital communication. Suddenly, we were selfie-obsessed. Just texts weren't good enough; we would always send each other pictures throughout the day. It took him a while to warm up to this, and at first, there were a lot more pictures coming from my end. He might send one half-ass blurry selfie in response to four from me in a given day. I doubt I need to explain the excitement of sharing selfies with someone you're into, but they just made the whole thing much more real. Like wow – you exist – and you are going out into the world, looking like you do in this picture, and you'll be talking to me all day in this outfit. Basic, basic puppy love stuff, but it was nice. So many days I lusted over his stupid expressionless face in a baseball hat.

As he started sending pictures, sometimes I found his style to be off base. The whole "fashion conscious sports guy" didn't always translate. Of course, at this time, I thought I was a little fashionisto, having spent thousands of dollars of disposable income on arcane brand name clothes throughout college. That was back when I was working full-time with no real debt. My point being, a lot of the photos he sent me actually turned me off a bit, and left me with a "please don't tell me you wore than in real life" sentiment. Again – completely shallow – but this is growing up, people.

The fact that I always felt that he had the upper hand in the relationship helped me see past some of these pitfalls. What was I going to do, tell my straight curious dream man he didn't know how to dress? I wasn't about to piss off my only source of happiness and excitement. If one picture was a turnoff, I would refresh my memory with a cuter picture from our history and not mention it. I told myself, clothes don't make the man, Barney's makes the clothes that you can later buy and force the man to wear.

One particularly exciting aspect of Christian was that he always referred to me by a pet name of sorts. Most often, "punk." Now some of you may be wondering – is that really all that endearing? To me it was. It was a "straight" man expressing himself in the only way he knew. I was (and have always been) quite sarcastic, dramatic, and a smartass, so "punk" was actually spot-on. I was often poking fun at him or giving him a hard time. I must admit – even though I was often careful not to upset him or push too hard – he did understand my dry sense of humor, which is essential to longevity with me. Sure, he could have said something like "babe" or the like, but that's not really what we were and I doubt he nor I were at a stage where we would feel comfortable applying that word to a man.

In many ways, "punk" was my first example of a gay pet name, and I accepted it and strangely cherished it. Every time he used it, I knew we were on a good page. I guess it's like couples that use "babe" – you're generally not using it during a heated argument. It comes out when things are more or less stable and you are in a good place. Although I have a theory that people overuse "babe," especially when they are actually annoyed with one another and trying to soften statements that are intended to be hard blows. How many times have you overheard an argument at The Cheesecake Factory? "That's not what I meant at all *babe*, if you were listening you would have heard what I said but you have a listening problem…*babe.*" I honestly hate the word babe. At any rate, "punk" was more or less our code word for "babe," and it felt nice that our relationship was deepening into pet name territory.

It wasn't long before we wanted to Facetime one another. Yes – Facetime was available, this wasn't that damn long ago. I recall having talked to Christian on the phone a couple times, but it always left me with a weird vibe. For one, he was shy. And more significantly, this was a new world to both of us. It was fairly easy to communicate over text and jump a bit out of our comfort zone, but something about a phone call makes it reality. Something about actually having to use the words "I miss you" or "you look cute today" audibly makes it more gay than just typing it in a message. I recall endless silences the times we did try to have a phone conversation. The very silences that conveyed him as mysterious or shy were flat-out awkward as the timer on my early iPhone ticked.

Phone calls were complicated. You would think Facetime would amplify that complication, but actually seeing the person that you miss and think is cute serves as a distraction. An awkward silence on a phone call is just that – awkward. An awkward silence on Facetime (of which we had many), is staring at the person and making them laugh, or asking, "What are you looking at?" There's just more ways to make it fun and less uncomfortable. At the very least, I could imagine him naked if he was being stupid or quiet. So we started a nightly Facetime ritual, and we both became quite hooked. He still didn't talk a ton, and I was supporting most of the conversation, but he slowly opened up.

Virtual Insanity

One time I remember asking him why he even liked me – it was no doubt one of the times it felt like a struggle to get him to talk. He said, and I remember this exactly, "you came at me correct." What a "straight guy" way to say it – I thought it was so cute. He told me that other guys just wanted to see his nudes, or couldn't maintain a conversation. Funny, I thought – I have the same damn problem with you many times. But I understood what he meant. With us, it seemed like we started things off like a friendship. Sure, we were on Grindr (with its obvious sexual undertones) and we were also attracted to one another, but there was an above-board flirtation that went on for a while. That somewhat innocent flirtation was a foundation for us.

I think it was the perfect storm, I approached him based off of what he was giving me. I can't deny that there were times when all I wanted out of a guy was a nude – but if I had approached Christian on that level, he would have stopped responding and blocked me. I got that vibe from him early on, and that vibe is what kept me in the right lane and kept our relationship flowing. I had no trouble being respectful and getting to know someone on a deeper level. I guess I just never expected to find guys like that on Grindr, so I had started acting the way everyone was treating me (shortcut: that is literally the entire problem with Grindr, you can stop reading this book early and leave me an Amazon review).

But seriously – in dating, on Grindr or anywhere else, you really have to know your standards and goals and approach people in a way consistent with those. It's hard to stay focused, but most of my successful relationships or situationships came out of a steadily paced courtship process that, at its core, was respectful. I treated Christian like a person, which earned his respect and allowed him to open up to me. You never know what type of magical persona guys are hiding behind their "Grindr wall." Sometimes you just have to be patient and kind if you see something in someone. The forces of Grindr work as a direct antithesis to your patience, but if you stay strong you may encounter this surprisingly pleasant outcome.

That said, things weren't always perfect with Christian. So many aspects of him excited me and held my attention, but there were a number of issues as well. I guess in this era of Grindr, I didn't have room to be picky. Certainly, the good outweighed the bad with him, but part of me felt like this is "nice for now," but probably wouldn't work forever. Again, I wasn't looking for "forever" at this stage, but since I liked him so much, the thought crossed my mind. I often felt like I was a great fit for him, but he didn't realize the many incompatibilities I felt on my end.

Our personalities were just too different. Sometimes I would get tired of trying to get him to share or open up with me. When he did, it was rewarding, but I felt like it took too much work to get to that point. Sometimes, he wouldn't really understand my jokes. As I said, he got my sense of humor overall, but some of the disconnects we had were eye-opening. I guess I was more of a "Tumblr guy" around this time (who am I kidding, I just posted on my Tumblr today), and that lends itself to a whole early generation of memes and alternative, *Daria*-esque humor. That wasn't Christian at all. A lot of times I had to filter or translate the things I was trying to say before saying them, because I knew he wouldn't quite understand. In some ways, this disconnect was a challenge that kept me interested, but some days I was over it. A "haha" and "yeah" only goes so far to keep me engaged in a conversation. Reciprocation was not his biggest forte.

Up to now, I have conveniently glossed over the fact that we had progressed to the level of exchanging more suggestive photos (and Facetimes), often. This was Grindr in my early 20's people, that is so much of what it was about. In a lot of ways, that physical connection (albeit, digital) kept us interested in a way that far exceeded any issues we were beginning to notice. There was actually a sense of relief and comfort in having that more intimate connection with him. There's nothing like a fresh nude to negate an uncomfortably slow-moving conversation.

Instead of needing to fish for that type of attention from random strangers, Christian became my "sure thing" ready to go every night. You guys know – it takes a ton of work to find someone you vibe with in this way. It felt refreshing and exciting to have someone so into me (and vice versa). I think much of it was puppy love, and I would really describe what we had as an early infatuation. Whatever image we had built of one another in our minds was working. We looked right past the warning signs – awkward phone calls, hadn't met in real life. What we had was working, and it was consistent and great.

At some point, I feel like the suggestive photos and Facetimes hijacked our relationship a bit. Before, Christian was more of a friendship and someone to talk to. Once it got to a more intimate level, however, he seemed to demand more and more of that type of attention. I was happy to oblige – again, I was completely attracted to him. That said, I was starting to feel like our conversations were being replaced by nudes at an unsustainable rate. At what point does our solid connection become the prehistoric equivalent of an OnlyFans video stream?

From the beginning, I felt like he had the power in the relationship. This was true in the more intimate aspect of our communication too. Suddenly, he was demanding photos from me. I definitely played into the dynamic, because at the time it was exciting. I was thinking – ok – this is how it is with gay guys. I have to play this part and keep him happy. Hell, I found it somewhat soothing that he was taking the lead in all things sexual. I had no idea of what to expect or how these things were supposed to go in real life. Our dynamic continued to be fun and exciting, but a sliver of me wondered where he was going with this controlling thing. Were we losing the cool friendship component of our dynamic and did he actually respect or value me beyond this?

What used to be a "how was your day" started turning into a "you know what I want." In a way, it was flattering and fun, but it also diminished the mental component of it – which, although weak, was crucial in differentiating Christian from any other guy on Grindr. I was playing a part to keep it going, and I still feared the potential loneliness of pissing Christian off and losing him altogether. Reflecting back, I wonder how much of Grindr culture had influenced Christian, even in these early years. Ultimately, if you met a guy from Grindr, you knew he was down to or accustomed to these types of exchanges. In a way, our extended courtship helped us develop a trust and foundation, but we seemed to be throwing it away by reverting to a meaningless Grindr relationship. We established that we had the capability to be "better than" those other guys on Grindr, yet regressed to exactly that dynamic. Perhaps other factors were at play – namely, laziness or a creeping disinterest from one or both of us.

Caught Out There

By now it had been a couple months of interaction with Christian. Around this time, I vividly remember an uncomfortable "come to Jesus" moment in our relationship. We still hadn't met in person. We talked about wanting to, but I think both of us had some apprehension. Sure it would be exciting and potentially hot, but were we ready to translate all of the ways we communicated and lusted after one another in real life? I felt neither of us was ready.

We were in an advanced gay relationship via text, but the truth was that we were both awkward beginners with no concept of how to even *exist* around another gay man. That said, this whole time he knew where I lived (which was a massive apartment complex so I had no fear of being stalked or anything). I had a general idea of where he lived too. Point being, one day he texted me to say that he was literally two blocks away from my house. Apparently, he was at the wedding of a family friend at a banquet hall literally within view of my apartment.

I immediately panicked. We had talked about meeting, but I had no warning or ramp up period. I also had a roommate who didn't know about my sexuality. What was I going to do, invite him in? What do I introduce him as? "My friend who I met…at a sports game…because by the way I never told you this before but sports are enjoyable?" I was scrambling, but Christian really wanted to meet.

He was trying to calm me down. He claimed that he just

wanted to come by and say hi – and actually see me in person. I was nervous – and was not ignorant to the many meanings of a guy wanting to "come by and say hi." In this case, he literally probably wanted to just say hi (I doubt he could sneak out of the wedding for too long), but I still felt uncomfortable. Suddenly, this guy that was a fantasy would be in my personal space. This was the last bit of armor I had around myself and the idea that being gay was some secret that I kept locked behind my phone screen.

He started begging to come over, and I started to feel sick. I was facing the prospect of pissing him off and losing him entirely if I didn't meet. That was the last thing I wanted to happen, but also meeting him on this day under these circumstances was *also* the last thing I wanted to happen. So which last thing took precedent? It was a lose-lose. Ultimately, I declined his offer to meet.

I actually had to ignore his texts and throw my phone in a corner for a while so I wouldn't have to deal with the guilt. He was *right* there, why couldn't I just go outside and say hi? Why was this so stressful? I go outside all the time, and see people all the time. Here is one I really liked, what was going on with me? The feelings of gay guilt came rushing – this was something I clearly enjoyed and wanted to explore, but as soon as it became real I wanted to run away from it. I have to believe that almost all of us go through this, and it is simply a process. Maybe Christian was going to be the casualty of this process – someone that could have been great for me but who I wasn't ready to accept. I began to worry that I screwed the whole thing up.

After looking at my phone (hours later) and being greeted by a number of pissed off texts from him, I knew a lot of damage had been done. "WTF man" and "you're weak as fuck" was the general tone of how my decision made him feel. He couldn't believe that I wouldn't just meet him, especially since I was at home and we were rarely so close to each other (mind you, we lived about 15 minutes apart, so it wasn't impossible to meet on other occasions). In looking at the totality, it's shocking that I completely accepted the blame without once considering his high-pressure ultimatum as being uncool. I didn't once consider that he could have been more considerate knowing that we both were in a weird stage of our sexuality. I wonder how I would have felt if those "WTF" texts said, "hey man – I understand – it's a process and when the time is right we will meet."

You're Toxic

After this transgression of sorts, he kept talking to me, but the dynamic had definitely shifted. He started using this incident against me, like I constantly had something to prove to him now. He would always throw it in my face…"But remember when you didn't meet up with me?" I was willing to take it – I did feel guilty about it. I think the incident really messed with our power dynamic (in his mind). For so long, I was playing along with the idea of him being in control, but when push came to shove, I made the final call. He probably didn't like that. What he didn't understand was I was playing into his control for the purposes of the fantasy of our relationship, but don't get it twisted, I wasn't going to do anything I didn't want to – even if he *was* cute.

At this point, neither of us had really discussed "deleting the app" for one another, despite how close we had become. I would go on Grindr here and there and so would he, but after the incident of not meeting him, I felt like we were both on the app a lot more. We still texted, sent photos, and (eventually) Facetimed once I had somewhat gotten back into his good graces, but things weren't the same. The incident tainted the undertones of excitement and urgency that had gotten us this far. That said, he was still my best option – so we continued with this new dynamic.

I knew that I wasn't going to vibe (or even want to vibe) with anyone other than him, and I had to believe he felt the same way based on how frequently we still talked. We were still hooked on one another, and in a lot of ways he was basically a secret boyfriend that I was semi-frequently on the rocks with. But that drama and tension kept me hooked. Just like the initial challenge of getting him to open up, the challenge of making sure he still liked me captured a lot of my focus. Not healthy, again, but a distraction and something that I didn't mind playing into for the reward of his attention. "Reward" – sadly, a penis that texts you back is just like that free matcha latte at Starbucks. Nothing more than a pleasant surprise that you only receive in exchange for weeks of your obedient patronage.

The discussion of meeting up came up from time to time, but both of us seemed reluctant for various reasons. Sometimes I would express being ready, and he would act like I was going to ghost him and throw in my face the time we didn't meet. Sometimes he would be ready and I still felt uncomfortable actually going through with it. In short, we were a mess. Each of those failed attempts (or failed discussions) kind of took us down a level in our connection. What were we, really? We live in the same city, we're attracted to one another, we talk all the time – but we're kind of afraid to meet and default to exist in this digital fantasy of one another. I guess we were digital friends with benefits, and that was both the good and bad part of our relationship. Over time, we stopped taking one another seriously.

The photos continued, along with his controlling dynamic. Some months later, it was clear that both of us were on Grindr frequently, hoping we could find someone with the same connection, but without this extensive and awkward history. It was so much easier to start with someone fresh than to continue to hash out why we couldn't meet or take one another seriously. By now, Christian had morphed into a guy that I texted periodically – mostly late at night – as my "sure thing" for attention. He wasn't stupid; I was exactly the same thing to him. When we texted each other, we knew what we wanted. Like hey – we don't click on these other levels anymore but I'm still attracted to you and would rather do this weird digital benefits thing with you than these other losers. So we did just that. The pet name disappeared, and the relationship became pretty cold.

Back and Forth

Eventually, I would come across guys that did excite me in similar ways as Christian, and also ones that I had more of a mental connection with. Of course at those times, I felt completely fulfilled talking to the new guys, so I would completely ignore Christian. Like Jennifer Lopez to Mariah, I simply didn't *know* him. I'm sure he's a talented guy with a lovely penis but I just don't recall meeting him (this book continues to be a lamb only zone, sorry). Anyway, Christian would notice my tendency to completely drop him – and it wouldn't go over well. This began a destructive cycle for our relationship. Especially when my "new guys" ultimately wouldn't work out, and I would desperately hit Christian up for attention.

A lot of times, I would block him as I met a new guy that I was ready to take more seriously. This was not out of some hatred for Christian, but because I wanted to stop any temptation from me texting him, so I could focus on the new guy and move on. By now, some time had passed and I was more open in my gay journey to actually meet men and consider dates. It was weird, because why wouldn't I go back to Christian and give him a try? I guess too much had happened that I knew he would force me to overcome. Rather than beg to get back in his good graces with weeks of undoubtedly sultry photo shoots, I could be some new guy's *everything* immediately.

Christian noticed the several times I had blocked him (either on Grindr or on text), and took it very personally. I have to believe that he was also talking to new guys during these times (since we weren't talking to each other at all), but something about the "official block" was particularly cold to him. Sure, it is cold in general, so I understand. But he really didn't like my explanation of blocking him to focus on the new guys. I would try to level with him – wouldn't you want the same level of focus from a new guy you were dating? Or would you want him still hanging on to guys from his past? Of course, the context of these explanations to Christian would be when my "new guy" had already failed, and I'd have unblocked Christian to try to get his attention again.

That probably wasn't an ideal pattern or opportunity for me to explain away my sins, so to speak. But hey, I was immature in a world of early Grindr, trying to find the perfect situation for myself at any cost. I actually thought the blocking thing was mature for the purpose of putting my entire focus on the new guys, but I completely see (now) how it was also very hurtful to the guys I was throwing to the side. If I never came back to those guys again, it would be one thing, but to come back and open the same wound repeatedly was very problematic. *The same wound, Flav? You opened the same damn wound?* (Shout out to when New York lost *Flavor of Love* the second time).

Compromise was out of the question for me during these times – I wanted the new guy, and I wanted the old guy ready to go when the new guy didn't work out. I felt I deserved every option. It was reckless and ultimately damaging to myself. But on the Grindr loop of constant distraction, you often don't realize the damage you're doing. You so infrequently have to deal with yourself or just sit in the emotion of what you are feeling on Grindr. There is *always* someone to talk to next.

I feel like they should actually add a mandatory time-out feature. Like hey, you just met this great guy, if it doesn't work out you aren't allowed to come back for a month so you actually learn something from this. But that's not their business model, and when love and hookups are a business, feelings are just a line-item expense. There is a ton of damage in the gay community as a result. Sure, Grindr gave so many of us what we wanted, but it came at a cost. It changed the way we interacted with one another. It gave so many of us a ton of privilege, to pick and choose who we want as if we're more worthy of love than anybody else. It created expectations. Perhaps most damaging, the expectation that there is somebody else constantly ready to give you attention and that you never have to deal with your past if you don't want to.

Of course, with Christian, this cycle continued endlessly. I would find a guy to talk to and block him, it wouldn't work out, and I'd be back trying to get on his good side again. On the flip side, he started doing the same thing. When we would find someone new to talk to and if I messaged him in the interim (he wouldn't block me), it would be a "bro, I have a guy now I'm good." He loved being able to rub it in my face. The previous allure of his one-word responses so quickly transformed into just cold and disinterested one-word responses. Many of those times I'd desperately ask him what I could do to get back on his good side, only to be confronted by a "nah – I'm good."

Of course, sometimes the timing would align that both of us would be without a guy at the same time. Those were, of course, the most promising moments. It would be an instant rush talking to him again, and provided a false safety net from the reality of a Grindr crash. A "Grindr crash" being the feeling of *thinking* you found someone perfect to make up for all of your past mistakes and prevent you from needing to deal with those residual issues, only for it *not* to work out and for everything to come crashing down around you even harder. Right before I hit the pavement on so many of those Grindr crashes, Christian would be there with his texts to save me.

Sext Me Harder

This pattern dragged on endlessly. Literally, for years. Of course, during that time, my gay identity had evolved, I had come out to friends, I had experienced some more serious relationships, but one way or another, I would find myself on Grindr. Since neither Christian nor I ever moved too far away from LA at this time, we would always seem to run into each other online. In many ways, I considered Christian the quintessential "Grindr guy," and maybe I was just like him. He was *always* on Grindr. At least, when I ran into him on there.

I felt like no matter how hard he tried, he would just end up back on the app. Rather than relate to him (because I was in the exact same position), I judged him for it. I felt like it degraded his personal brand. I questioned why he was always on there. Was his pursuit of dick insatiable? Why would I ever want to settle down with the guy that other guys have talked to thousands of times and whose pictures have been sent all over the city? Again – totally judgmental and not cool (don't be all *uncool* – RHONY, anyone?), because I knew our shared intention was ultimately to get off of the app and find a good guy as soon as possible. Nonetheless, we were both addicted and not finding any luck. Perhaps it was a self-perpetuating issue. Were we not settling on a guy because we were addicted to the rush of talking to so many more? Or were we genuinely trying and not meeting our matches, ending up on the app out of loneliness and desperation?

The sad part of it all is although I never had Christian's name in my phone, I had seen his number on my screen so many times that I eventually memorized it. Blocking was useless, because all I would do was find his number on my block list, unblock it, and text him when I needed to. Sometimes I would forget a digit or two, and dig desperately in any history I had to try to find it and get my rush of talking to him. I was literally addicted to the attention like a drug. I would pull up my Sprint bill from prior years (yes Sprint, judge me), and dig through the numbers hoping to find a month where we had an awkward phone conversation (since iMessages don't actually show up on your bill). Or similarly embarrassing, I would dig through old texts on my MacBook, since they wouldn't delete at the same time as when I removed his texts from my phone. It was desperate, but when I needed Christian, I would get a hold of Christian one way or another.

Sometimes our reconnections would be ok, but many times they would be toxic. The guy was completely over me, but how would you feel if a guy you once liked quite a bit kept coming back to you? I guess part of him always held hope that something was there

– and honestly, I did too. Immediately after the many mistakes made with my "new guys," I would reflect fondly on our connection. Of course, hindsight erases all of the bad memories or issues you had with the person. You immediately latch onto the good times, the amazing connection, and just want to get back to that level.

I would be so satisfied once I got Christian texting me again semi-frequently. Even though it took work and time, it was so much more safe and comfortable than trying to build that connection with someone new. There was no need for small talk, we knew each other and what we wanted – attention and fun. Sometimes it would take weeks for me to get back into his good graces, but I always was up for the challenge. Once I got his attention back, I knew I could maintain it. We would continue on sometimes for weeks, or sometimes days before I would just get over him and move on again. In a lot of ways, I guess it was a game of conquest for me. Could I get him back this time, after the exponentially increasing failures? For him, I think he was enjoying the façade of control I was giving him each time, which was required to get him back.

It became a twisted game of – ok, you want my attention again? You have to do this, or send me this, or say this. A lot of times, it made me feel worthless and beneath him. Sure, it used to be exciting – this weird control dynamic, but it felt wrong that I had to work so hard just to have someone talk to me again. What did I expect? I treated him like garbage when I didn't need him, and he was treating me like garbage when I needed him back. The right thing to do for both of us would be to cut it off, but we continued. I knew that on any of these tries, I could have genuinely focused my attention on him and given us an actual shot again, but I felt that too much damage had been done. I continued to feel a mental disconnect with him, and thought that I would eventually find someone I connected with more easily on that level. With Christian, it was purely a distraction of physical attraction.

<u>See You Again</u>

On one of these many "reconciliations," I actually met Christian in real life. Yes, even after a couple years of back and forth, we hadn't actually met. Of course, during this period I had met countless guys so that initial nervousness over meeting Christian was a distant memory. If I had a gluten free cookie for every Netflix and chill I'd been a party to by now I'd be *Angelica Pickles in West LA: The Movie*. At this point, I had my own place downtown so my setup was ideal for these last minute rendezvous. I forget the exact circumstances, but I think Christian had just finished a hike or workout and was in my area. I only found out because I randomly texted him out of boredom. We had been texting infrequently in the weeks prior after (of course) coming across one another on Grindr.

The whole thing was a bit anti-climactic in how quickly it happened. We were definitely worthy of an episode of *Catfish* at this point. I needed at least 6 cameras in a public park to capture the very real potential for this to go horribly wrong. I texted him my address and in pure Christian fashion, he said "k." I was wondering whether he meant "k" as in he was on his way or "k" as in, noted, but not coming right now. Well, ten short minutes later the mystery was solved when he texted me "here." I started my journey to the lobby of my building – my heart was suddenly racing. This was the exact moment that I had avoided years ago, and now I had become a willing participant. Is this going to be some revenge moment for him or an ability to finally cuss me out in person? Our conversations had been neutral up to this point – so I doubted that outcome.

I opened the front door of my building and looked around the corner. There he was, exactly as I had always imagined. Sure, we had countless photo and FaceTime references of one another, but it still felt comforting that he was exactly as expected after so much time. There was Christian, right in front of my face. I remember this moment fondly, because he was wearing a workout outfit, similar to the original faceless photo that attracted me to him to begin with. I said "hey" and we engaged in an awkward hug, as he followed me inside. No major proclamations of "oh my God" or "finally" – he was acting as though we met on Grindr 20 minutes before. It was really strange that it happened so easily (given our history), but maybe we both just wanted to get it over with and see who this person was after so much time.

He came inside, and it was very weird for an extended period. We didn't know our in-person dynamic. We had been texting infrequently in the weeks up to this, so it wasn't some big culmination to this in-person moment. We weren't head over Nike Flyknits for one another; we probably just had no one better to talk to at the time. It was just another one of our texting cycles, except here he was, live and in color. It was really hard to hold a conversation with him – some things never change. It was one of those "God I almost wish you weren't here" moments, except it wouldn't end. The excitement of him finally being in my face faded much more quickly than anticipated. Undoubtedly, his approach was "well, here I am," show me why you want to hang out so bad. Of course, in-person I was not the subservient texter he had grown accustomed to over the years. I was fully out now, I dated now, I went to dinners – I expected the basics, like conversation.

The mood was uncomfortable. We weren't talking much, the show we were watching wasn't entertaining, and neither of us seemed to want to be there but didn't know how to end it in a remotely comfortable manner. We just kept watching TV in relative silence. I'd ask him a question here or there, and he would directly respond, quickly reverting us back into silence. Eventually he moved closer to me on the couch and made a move (thank God, because I had no idea how to transition the moment other than a hook up or by kicking him out).

I wasn't actually expecting anything that day, I thought maybe we'd hang out, and it if it wasn't completely horrible, we'd hang out more or even go on a date or something. He had other intentions, clearly, or ran out of options as things became more awkward. We finally hooked up that afternoon. I felt conflicted about the whole thing – from when he made the move to when it progressed. This isn't what I necessarily wanted, I was open to it, but it almost felt like a conquest thing. Like we don't connect and we both know it, but I can still get you to hookup with me. It definitely wasn't natural, but I played into it mostly out of my own curiosity. There was definitely a physical connection there and I would say it was a good hookup, but the aftermath was so completely awkward. That tends to be the case when you wait so long to meet someone.

I can tell that hooking up that afternoon was all we would ever accomplish. As soon as it was over, he said he needed to go and I gladly showed him out of the door. "I can have another you in a minute, 'matter fact he'll be here in a minute." Kidding, I had no appointments lined up after him but I *could* have. I had no idea where his head was. Did he enjoy it, did he just want to get it over with and never speak again? He didn't completely ghost me afterwards, but I remember the conversation quickly fell off after then. We texted in the following days but that lag (as most of you know) is far too much time after a hookup if something more was to come of it. If that shit goes well, you're texting within the next couple hours. If you would rather forget about it, you will never text again. If it was not as expected but you don't completely hate the guy, sure, you might respond to a text from him in the coming days – we were that last outcome.

Clearly this hookup was either a final step for him with me, or something didn't go the way he expected. I really didn't mind or sit around feeling any type of sadness afterward. I said the hookup was good, not *amazing*. He was cute that day, but so many of our potential differences were also readily apparent. For one, he was completely more shy and uncomfortable than I expected him to be, especially with the advantage of years since our initial meeting. Perhaps I had matured more quickly into my gayness than he? Or perhaps our awkward history was too much for him to get over and talk to me like a normal guy would. Either way, I didn't feel like dating would work out amazingly for us, but again, I was open to my mind being changed after that encounter (although I severely doubted it). I had nothing else going on, you never know.

Eventually, time went on and our communication completely fell off. After this hookup with Christian, I had a couple other short relationships and situationships. The more I matured, the longer these relationships would last and the more distance I built between Christian and me in my mind. After a 3 or 6-month relationship, I wouldn't suddenly find myself alone and longing for Christian. Perhaps that last hookup became a vivid memory in my head of why it would never work. I didn't have any tangible evidence like that before, only my idealized image of our amazing puppy love connection. Another almost two years went by before I ever really thought about Christian again.

One More Chance

After more or less two years passed, I found myself as lonely as I was on that first night I ever spoke to Christian. It's no coincidence that Grindr always leaves you in the same position. Here I was, once again, looking for someone to talk to. This time, I was in a new city entirely, maybe 20 miles away from downtown. I scroll and scroll, and I see Christian, face picture and all. So much time had passed since that final (and only) hookup, and it was really nice to see his face again. We had never had a definitive issue after that day, the conversation simply fell off. I messaged him and wondered if he would even reply – perhaps he was actually done with me just as I figured I was with him (until I saw him, that is).

I didn't get an immediate response, but he did reply eventually. It turns out that after all this time, we were actually living in the same city – a few miles from each other. I wondered what the odds were on that. He seemed to have come along nicely in life. He had moved out from his family's house into a place of his own, had a new job, seemed more mature and independent, and was religiously into cross-fit. I couldn't lie and say that wasn't all attractive to me (well, I'm not for the cult of cross-fit but if it makes you look bomb I will accept that residual benefit). The awkwardness of that last meeting became a distant memory when I realized that the *new* Christian might have leveled up into the type of guy I typically have interest in (so long as he spoke now). We talked on and off over the course of a couple weeks. Of course, here we were meeting on Grindr once again. It really sparked that former notion of him being the "Grindr guy." It takes one to know one, I guess.

It was clear that Christian was keeping his distance at this point. Our conversation was empty, a vague catching up with one another that he responded to when he felt like. Part of me really wanted to see him again. One, because I was lonely – and two, because the idiotic romantic in me thought there was some sort of broader reason the universe had brought us to the same place. Ok, I wasn't in *that* deep, but I just thought we could probably get along and be friends, if not friends with benefits in this new phase of life.

About two weeks later, pretty late at night, he invited me over. Notably, we had gone through a significant back and forth of meeting at his place or my place. I wanted him to come to my place (perhaps out of sheer laziness), but he refused to. At the same time, he was hesitant to invite me to *his* place. Maybe he didn't want his new environment to be tinged by the ghost of Grindr past. I was getting annoyed with the drama of it and the fact that our destiny to meet was completely under his control (per usual).

When I finally got his invite, despite being tired, I knew I had to take it or the opportunity might not come around again. No worries – I could study for my life-determining bar exam later. I parked outside of his building and texted him…"here." His place was really cute, and he was looking good himself. I was wholly impressed with this current version of him. He showed me around, and we eventually landed on his couch and watched *Love and Hip Hop*. Wow, I thought, I wish I knew you liked this back then. We would have had something to connect on for the past 4 years. At the very least, I would have put it on during our awkward hookup years ago.

We watched the show and actually laughed and talked a bit. Maybe he had matured into more of a conversationalist, or maybe so much time had passed that things weren't weird between us anymore. Perhaps Momma Dee (Lil Scrappy's mother on the show) has a way of breaking the ice that neither of us could accomplish on our own. I'll never know, but it was nice catching up with him, and for the first time, I felt like I was just his friend. Nothing ultimately happened that night. I was there for about an hour, and then I decided to leave. It was nice to see him, but something about our vibe wasn't there to support the potential romantic or physical ideals I had in the back of my mind. For countless reasons we both knew, our relationship had run its course. I'm not sure why he allowed me to come over that night – perhaps my persistence always broke him down. I figured, if he knew he was done with me, this wouldn't even have happened.

Perhaps Christian was open to a check-in every couple years to explore the potential. Most likely, we both had developed a soft spot for one another after years of interaction. Nonetheless, a potential beyond friendship was not there. It felt good to see him one last time, and almost served as a "no hard feelings" for the extensive back and forth our relationship had endured. We were truly kids, figuring this shit out when we first met. We had a great connection, it got weird, it got toxic, it felt nice at times, and texting probably both saved us the grief of a bunch of random hookups over the years. Despite the control issues we had, I fully believe that Christian matured into a special guy that will no doubt be a great husband to someone one day (or hell, maybe already is). I'd call this one a Grindr draw.

[7] WHAT CHRISTIAN TAUGHT ME

So many aspects of my attraction to Christian boiled down to fantasy – the version of him I had built in my head. That is a recurring theme with my experience on Grindr, and likely, with our collective experience of meeting men digitally. I covered a bit of this earlier, when discussing online "stats" and how we perceive them as exciting. But I think there's more to unearth on that topic. So many of us claim to be fair and equal opportunity when it comes to dating, but at the end of the day, attraction is a human trait. By human, I mean that it is imperfect, unfair, and biased. Attraction is so many different things – it is mental, physical, emotional, and spiritual. Without question, it is layered, and any person can be attracted to one or multiple aspects of another.

What I'm getting at, however, is that physical attraction almost always has to be there for a relationship to commence and succeed. Where "stats" come into that discussion is that Grindr has taken an already cutthroat system of being judged on physical attraction and made it even worse. Before, we would look at someone in life, perhaps appreciate some aspects of their physical appearance and find issue with others. We would look at a photo or two, and sometimes be conflicted about whether or not someone was cute to us in just *one photo*, or all the time. Perhaps we found them more attractive when they smiled, or when they were making a funny face. There was some wiggle room, some interpretation – essentially, there was a chance for everyone to perceive others in a slightly thoughtful manner, given that judging others purely on appearance is already pretty brutal. But then came Grindr and "stats." Suddenly, your physical appearance is coupled with baseball-card-like statistics on where you stack up in the gay universe.

Almost immediately, there is a fierce amount of judgment on who you are and what your "gay value" is. There is an insane amount of focus on age, weight, and height. Think about that – the three aspects of people that are, for better or worse, unchangeable are the three aspects that suddenly define one's online worth. Sure, pre-Grindr dating focused on these traits as well, but it was far less brutal. For instance, most people wouldn't really know the age of someone before speaking to them in a bar. On Grindr, you are able to filter out a potential match based on some cutoff in your head. "No one over 27 is going to work for me." Ok – did you just leave out the 29 year old of your dreams? How would you ever know?

It doesn't stop there. Suddenly, below 5'10" is your arbitrary cutoff for height you're interested in. Are you telling me that in real life, if you were attracted to a guy across the street, you would be able to tell me whether or not he was 5'9" or 5'10"? Then we get to weight. Suddenly, 200 pounds is a bit too heavy for your taste. Would you really be able to tell if the attractive barista at your local coffee shop is 190 vs. 200 pounds? On Grindr, everything boils down to numbers and cutoffs. Some people don't even look at photos – they subconsciously skim your photo and get right to the stats. It has become ingrained in us – it doesn't matter how you look, the stats have to be desirable. If your stats don't match the Grindr-facilitated "dream player" men have created in their mind, you are out of the running – *even* if they think you are cute in your photo.

This type of judgment was otherwise impossible before Grindr, but now it is completely the norm. In fact, the more we use apps, the more our eyes gravitate to these types of statistics. Furthermore, we continue to build in our head the idea of the stats we think are worthy of our attention. Simply because we can, and because there are so many men to choose from to satisfy our appetites. If we all take an honest look at ourselves, almost all of us have been guilty of this in some fashion. I'm not saying that we should all be attracted to every single guy on Grindr. Physical attraction is already a merciless natural process.

What I am pointing out is that Grindr has basically used technology and data to enable the gay community (already quite image-focused) to make a bad situation worse. Suddenly, we have all of this information at our fingertips and create our own arbitrary statistics of what is desirable or beautiful, most of the time for no reason other than because we can. "Well, when I put my height cutoff at 5'10," I see more guys than I even have time to talk to, so I don't need to consider anyone below." Like children locked in a candy store – why would you even need to consider a vegetable? The candy might make you feel like shit and a vegetable is probably better for you, but right now, you are tunnel vision on these red vines. Gluttonous is truly the only word to describe the process.

But it doesn't stop there. We also have a user-created lexicon of descriptive terms, "soft stats" if you will, that evoke desire. I'm talking about terms like "hung," without a doubt. How many times have you been desperate to talk to anyone on Grindr? You come across some guys that don't seem to be your type, but at least they're online, and they have something like "hung" or "very hung" on their profile. Suddenly, this guy that you wouldn't give the time of day is "good enough" for your attention because you might get a nice dick pic out of it. And don't think that the guys who get less attention on Grindr aren't hip to this concept, and who can blame them? They use the words that they know will get them more attention, regardless of whether or not they identify with those terms. I mean who even defines what hung means? It is the epitome of "stat culture" – the idea that a number, measurement, or word makes you more desirable in the heartless world of instant and blind judgment that is online dating. Of course, the terms don't stop there; you have "VGL" (very good looking), "masc," "toned," "fit" – a slew of arbitrary concepts that people assign to themselves under the notion that it makes them more desirable. And it works.

It will likely take decades to undo the damages of "stat culture." These figures, terms, and in turn, our community's behavior, have created a new frontier for dating. Suddenly, every single person is empowered to have arbitrary, numbers-based expectations for what they deserve. Not only are these people damaging themselves (by cutting out men who are likely very well-suited to them in multiple ways), but they are also making thousands of men who do not happen to fall into their arbitrary cutoffs for attraction feel "less than." Now, for this, I can already hear the typical dissent – it's not my responsibility to be attracted to everyone or to make them feel good. That is true – I agree. But we must take accountability and acknowledge that this entire system of judgment is unhealthy and unfair for our community as a whole. Why does the so-called "elite's" pursuit of one another based on "premium stats" necessitate that so many others feel excluded and unworthy of affection? Is one man's pursuit of love more worthy than anyone else's?

There are, of course, many better ways to do online dating. I hope more of those approaches will surface with time, and maybe (just maybe) Grindr with its ubiquity can embrace some of those changes. For instance, disallowing people to filter based on unchangeable stats. Age, height, race, weight – is it too much of an inconvenience for hot guys to even *see* guys outside of their self-adopted stat requirements? What kind of message are we sending to guys that are screwed over by this shallow process – you just aren't good enough? Your race and weight aren't *in* this season? It's messed up and frankly, unacceptable.

I think we should also see more dating services that connect people based on shared interests before even revealing their pictures to one another. Sure, physical attraction will eternally play a role, but you will undoubtedly meet men you might not have chosen for yourself who would be great for you using this type of system. So many of the qualities and traits we choose as our "requirements" in online dating are out of technical necessity – they are *making* me choose an age range, a distance, and judge them based on a photo. I bet a lot of people would be open to trying some new and less judgmental ways to meet people, considering the system we have is not ideal (for examples of failures, see: this book you are currently reading, and part 1 of it). I believe everyone deserves love with a person they are attracted to, and I also believe that we don't need to make thousands of people still looking for love feel like shit during that process.

On the personal level, I think that each of us can improve this miserable "stat culture" by taking a look at how and why we judge others using stats. What perceptions of desirability has "stat culture" embedded in your head – and why do you abide by them? Why have you assigned value to words like "hung" or "muscular?" Do you immediately relate them to images of hot men in your head? How many times have you seen those words or met up with a guy *using* those words to find out your perception of them was incorrect? After all, these are subjective words that are open to interpretation. One man's muscular is another man's scrawny. The point is – these descriptions, these statistics and figures, hold far too much meaning in our pursuit of romantic connections.

Challenge yourself to interact with people regardless of these stats – you'll be surprised at the types of connections you make. Better yet, if you have been using some "deal breaker" stats, and I know height is a big one – challenge yourself to cast a wider net. You might not be finding a potential match because you are far too specific in whom you will accept, and for no substantiated reason other than vanity. "Well I like tall guys." Ok – have the last five tall guys you dated worked out for you? Think about the type of values you are prioritizing in dating – height is not going to text you and ask you how your day went – it is not going to keep you warm at night. Hung is not going to be there when you're sick or support you accomplishing your goals. Try to incrementally take some focus off of stats in your pursuit of great connection, and you may find it sooner than you think.

Moving on from stats to a pervasive issue with Christian and throughout both books of this series – blocking. Although I can't blame Grindr or even Apple for the advent of blocking, it seems that it really gained steam alongside the early Grindr years. Sure, I feel like MySpace had a blocking feature, but it's safe to say we have only grown more finicky since the early days of social media. Now more than ever, we have endless digital options on filtering out specific content. We pick and choose what we will tolerate on our feeds, and ultimately, whether or not we need to erase someone from our consciousness with a block.

Blocks aren't all bad, though, they have a lot of productive purposes. If you just went through a break up and know that you tend to go back to people who aren't good for you, a block might keep you focused on moving forward. A block on social media might prevent you from stalking exes, or from them stalking you. Sure, blocks are as easily undone as they are put in place, but the extra steps involved give you some time to remember why you blocked in the first place.

With Christian and so many of these guys, the core of my blocking was well intentioned. I never considered myself a shady blocker – I wasn't out to "cancel" these guys or get back at them for something. Most often, I blocked guys because I knew that I was frequently tempted to go back to them for attention, even after confirming the relationship wouldn't work out for various reasons. I blocked to prevent them from inadvertently riding on the roller coaster of communication that is "Lex." I blocked to prevent myself from reaching out during lonely moments, in the middle of the night, and restarting an endless cycle of communication that would ultimately go nowhere. The problem was, I also unblocked – frequently. I was obviously in a mature and solid place when I would institute these blocks. Perhaps I was talking to someone new and exciting, or felt like I had my act together and didn't care about dating.

Sooner or later, though, I would hit an extremely weak point. I knew exactly why I had blocked these guys, but that reason would not outweigh my immediate desire for attention from them. This plays into the issues of instant gratification that many of us grew accustomed to because of apps like Grindr. There is always someone online willing to give you the attention you need. With unblocking, I was seeking that same instant gratification, but was also greedy enough to want it from someone that I had dismissed in the past.

To be clear, these guys weren't angels either (a couple were, though). But in general, blocks were being thrown out left and right and are probably being used more than ever. There is nothing more offensive or triggering than finding out you are blocked, and that was ultimately a problem I had to face when unblocking these guys. I had to hear so much shit from them before they would even consider engaging with me again. In a twisted way though, that challenge of getting them to like me again was also gratifying to me. I would do whatever I needed to do, get the attention I needed from them again, and block them again once I was ready to move on.

So what is to blame for this cycle? Am I some evil person? I guess it depends on who's reading. There are layers of issues going on here. For one, I had good intentions, but couldn't carry them through. Another issue was the culture of instant gratification and always expecting there to be someone to talk to. Just sitting with your thoughts and taking some time off to reflect didn't even seem like an option with Grindr culture. It was always "what's next?" Of course, I also can't dismiss that I was a young man, trying to figure myself out and didn't have the level of maturity I do now. Perhaps I needed to be burned by multiple guys doing the same things I did to others before I realized how much it sucked. And trust me, I have been. I can't undo those years or those behaviors, but I learned a ton from them – and maybe this book is my big "sorry I wasn't better" to anyone I undoubtedly treated poorly in this digital conquest for affection.

What I will advise about blocking (and unblocking) is this.

These are powerful tools and we all have to remain cognizant that they don't only impact us. It is so easy to hit block and pretend someone doesn't exist, but depending on the reasons, it may or may not be the appropriate thing to do. A lot of times a block allows us to escape some uncomfortable conversation or confrontation with someone that might provide you (and them) with a level of productive understanding. "Hey, I'm so sorry, but I am going through some shit and it was really nice to talk to you tonight, but I have no idea what I want and am just going to waste your time, so I think it's best we part ways." That would provide a lot more insight to the recipient than just blocking them, and having them wonder for days what they did wrong or why they weren't good enough. They might be upset in the moment, but they will be better off knowing. That's not to say every block requires an explanation – if someone is being inappropriate, abusive, or otherwise driving you insane, a block is probably more productive than getting into a fight with them about the reasons.

Unblocking is even trickier. There is almost never a good reason for unblocking someone unless a ton of time has passed since you have blocked them (as in, years). If you find yourself wanting to unblock someone, take yourself back to the time and place when you actually blocked them. Feel those feelings. Reflect on why you thought this person would be someone you never wanted to communicate with again. That is a strong action you took, and it's going to be very unsettling for them to suddenly hear from you.

Even if they accept you reaching out positively, or there is some sudden rush or euphoria, it so rarely works out the way you intend. If you really want to unblock someone, I would also ask a few friends or family familiar with the person and your situation. Often, when thinking with the heart, it is impossible to make a sound decision. If more than one person reminds you why it's not a good idea to unblock and deal with this situation again – they are almost always right. Now, if years have passed and you might want to clear your conscience or be cordial with someone, you have a different situation. Again, it's probably better to leave things where they are, but I understand not wanting to have all of those negative demons (if they indeed haunt you). The point is – with blocking and unblocking – be thoughtful. Thoughtful of why you're doing it, whether it is unjustifiably hurtful to the other person, and why you should stick to it once you do it.

A minor point that is tangential to blocking is the idea of nostalgia. This was clearly going on throughout my interactions with Christian and pretty much every other guy in this series. You always reflect more fondly on a situation after some time has passed. Time has a way of erasing even substantial issues and annoyances you felt with a person, leaving you to fixate on what was amazing about them. In these cases, nostalgia is simply a side effect of loneliness and a lack of other options. Trust me, as soon as you find someone new to focus your attention on, you magically stop fixating on that ex you couldn't get your mind off for weeks. We've all been there. Not to say that feelings of nostalgia aren't valid – they are just often biased toward the outcome that you want in your head. You feel lonely, you miss your exes, so your mind (as your eternal ride-or-die teammate) begins fixating on everything amazing about your ex, because all you want is to feel those feelings again.

For nostalgia, I will say this. Try to keep it in check. Try to remind yourself of the full picture of the situation, rather than only the positives. Give it some time. The tendency is to give into your desires and reach back out to the person you're nostalgic about, but be patient. It might feel like torture, but you are often saving yourself some grief. For one, you cut this person off (or they cut you off), so even though you are thinking all of these amazing things about them – they might not share the same feelings. You might be greeted with a very unfriendly conversation, and instantly regret reaching out (this has happened to me many times).

Also, put yourself out there with new friends, projects, hobbies, and even potential new matches. Nothing kicks nostalgia's ass more than a busy scheduled and a busy mind. And, just like blocking, run your "nostalgia plan" by friends or family familiar with the relationship. They often do a great job of giving you a reality check. I'm not saying nostalgia never works out – sometimes the other person misses you too. But ultimately, if the core of your issues with someone were never worked on or addressed, nostalgia will only get you so far. It won't be too long before you're dealing with the same problems and reminded why the situation was never right to begin with.

It's hard to ignore that between all of this blocking and nostalgia with Christian, another constant was at play. The fact that I was constantly talking to other men on Grindr (and so was he). In fact, since we were never in any level of commitment, both of us were still on Grindr throughout even the good times of us knowing one another. When things were great between us, I suspect we were each on there less frequently, but the option for more Grindr attention remained. This raises a big issue. How can you ever give anyone a fair shot or the proper attention they probably deserve if you are constantly distracted by other guys and messages?

I recall many nights on Grindr when my profile was "on fire." I was maintaining fast-paced conversations with four or five guys, all of them equally attractive and seemingly into me. I'm a good multi-tasker, but after a while, my conversation with one or two of these guys really took off and the others fell off. Perhaps someone sent me a more exciting picture than another, or one guy lived closer or had more things in common. It was impossible to keep it all straight, and it was all very much like a game of whack-a-mole. Dick pic here, respond to him, cuss him out, tell older doctor guy what city you live in, explain to shirtless Hollywood actor what you do for a living, oops forgot to ask mysterious college student about his sexual preferences, but right before I ask sexy personal trainer what restaurant he wants to meet me at.

It is exhausting, and frankly, unfair to everyone involved. Sure, a lot of these guys are looking for casual encounters and conversation and won't take a lack of attention personally, but it really adds up. Let's say some of my conversations from "on fire" nights fell off, and I reach out to the ones I started ignoring the next day. If they are smart, they might realize "hey, this guy was online all last night but just not responding to me, and now he has the time of day – am I a second tier bitch to him?" I know I've felt that way about guys who did that to me. Grindr provides a constant rush and distractions – if you are on the app you are opening up yourself to even more distraction. By the way, while you're talking to these four or five guys, most of us are *still* scrolling on the app and looking for even *more* guys. We know the statistics – most of these conversations will fall off or go nowhere, so you need a pipeline of men to talk to when that happens.

The whole thing is ridiculous, but that's how Grindr's creators intended it to be. For them, the longer you are on the app, the more money they can make. They get to tell their advertisers they have a captive audience of gay men from 18-60 literally posted on this app all day who will see your pop-ups and advertisements whether they like it or not because they are addicted. Forget what it's doing to all of their self-esteem and mental health, as long as they are on there all the time. They are on there during work, while they're driving, while they're sleeping, at school.

Grindr comes first; life is almost secondary to it. And the whole system is created purposefully to hook you into always wanting something more or wondering what hot guy is around the corner. So even if you do meet someone successfully through the app (which they claim is their goal), your brain is so hooked on constant stimulation that you will subconsciously mess up your relationship or end it just to get back on the app and tap back into the constant stream of attention you are subconsciously hooked on. Grindr's favorite users are guys in open relationships (no disrespect or judgment to those guys), because for better or worse, it's a customer base that never actually has to leave the app.

How can you combat this issue and give the guys you're talking to a fair chance? Well, you have to be stronger than the extremely addictive system that Grindr has created. If you genuinely want to have a substantial relationship with someone (whether it is boyfriend, friendship, or anything else), you need to give them a certain level of focus. Create rules for yourself. Perhaps if you are talking to one guy you really like on Grindr, stop yourself from messaging or responding to messages from others. I know it is tempting, especially when cute guys message *you* and you don't want to miss the opportunity, but sometimes you have to. Reassure yourself by the fact that they will almost always still be there should the one guy you're talking to not pan out.

Another option is to start texting the one guy you are interested in to get the conversation off of the toxicity of the app and redirect your focus. Of course, you can't do that instantly and have to bring it up when you feel it's appropriate – but it's much easier to avoid the app altogether when you're trying to focus on someone. Constantly remind yourself – the rush of Grindr and the constant attention from it is most often empty and damaging. Eventually the attention fades, you run out of guys to talk to, and you're left there staring at a pointless grid. Don't let the Grindr "on fire" nights go to your head – they don't last forever. The bulk of these Grindr guys are not going to enhance your life – so when you find one that actually sparks your interest, give that guy the focus he deserves so the relationship actually has a chance. Hopefully he does the same – and if not, maybe you can raise that concern (when appropriate).

Throughout the Christian story, I also mentioned this idea of me perceiving him as just another "Grindr guy." Someone I would constantly see on the app, whose value I perceived as lower because he was always online, talking to a ton of guys. And, as mentioned before, he could probably say the same about me over the years. This very much correlates to the idea of "having too many notches in your belt," or perceiving people who have too many sexual partners as tainted goods. I attribute this line of thinking to my own elitism and immaturity at the time. Obviously, I knew that I was no better than the behaviors I was judging Christian for.

The bigger picture here is, these days most people are going online to find love. It is a convenience and almost necessity of modern society, which demands a whole lot from all of us and leaves very little time for us to do the things we want. There should be no shame or stigma around using Grindr or any other dating app – we all have needs and as long as we are being respectful of others along the way, we can fulfill those needs in any way we want. *We're all grown here.* If I throw it back to Kamran (for a moment), I have met guys over the years who I would later find out knew him and would say "oh he stays on Grindr," implying that he's some kind of Grindr whore. Those guys were no better than me with Christian – we have to stop the judgment. For a lot of us, Grindr is our only feasible way to meet and connect with gay men throughout the day. We shouldn't be judged for a desire to connect (in whatever way) with our community. So let's cut that out.

Another concept I'd like to reflect on with regard to Christian is the idea of how I approached him. Very early in our courtship, he acknowledged that he began to open up to me and liked me because I approached him from a respectful place. This causes me to reflect on the countless times I didn't approach men who may have been really great connections for me from the same place. For whatever reason – it was late at night, I was lonely, I had just gone through a break up, I was mad and destructive. At various points along my personal and emotional journey, I met a similar sample of men on Grindr – some really great for me and some definitely not for me. Depending on how I approached them, I became one of the two for *them* as well. It's not always how you look, what your stats are, or how close you live to a guy (if you'll believe me). I think each of us has a cross-section of men on dating apps that we are potentially compatible with. It might not be big – but there are a handful that could probably end up as our boyfriends depending on timing and chemistry.

One huge part of that chemistry is how we approach these guys *when* we cross paths. While we can't control what they're going through on their end (i.e. they could also be fresh out of a break up, lonely, etc.), we can control our approach to them and increase our odds for sustaining a meaningful connection. How do you accomplish this? Most often just patience and respect. Talk to these guys like you would talk to them in real life. Don't let the Internet's shield of anonymity embolden your hoeishness and demand a dick pic in the first 5 minutes (even if it's what you want, and sometimes that's fine).

If you really think someone might be a good candidate for dating or more than just a Grindr random, engage in conversation with them. Ask questions about them; don't just default to talking about yourself. Be charming, be funny, be sarcastic – highlight your personality. Don't complain or rant about everything – show some positivity. We all have a ton to complain about, but that's not the most attractive way to lead with a guy. Muster up all of your strength and try not to act jaded about dating (even though almost all of us are). It's really not attractive to talk to an otherwise great guy who just laments about how everyone is gross and how hard it is to find a match. Fact check – *your attitude* might be gross. I guess what I'm perhaps regretting a bit are the many times that I wasted an opportunity to get to know a great guy. So much of it boils down to your attitude and how you engage with them, and you have complete control over that. I guess this lesson is to "come correct" if you actually want someone.

My final lesson from Christian is the idea of control. As I mentioned throughout the story, many times I felt that he had a power over our relationship. I always somewhat feared that he would run away or that I would lose him if I didn't do what he was asking. Much of this took on the form of suggestive texts and the like, where he would start demanding things of me. In a way, I was attracted to this dynamic with him (for a while), but I later came to resent it because it was all he ever wanted and it never felt right to begin with. I'm no sex therapist (nor a therapist at all), but I'm sure there are healthy ways to explore a "control dynamic" or whatever the professional term is that I suggest you research before engaging in one.

For me, the lesson here is to just be aware that what seems like fun or innocent flirtation at first, could actually be someone manipulating you to get what they want. When you find yourself in this sort of control dynamic, it needs to be something that both parties are engaging in from a mutual understanding and level playing ground. You can't just be doing it to please the other person. I thought I was playfully allowing Christian to think he was the more dominant and controlling member of our relationship. But there isn't really a difference between faking submission and actual submission. I handed over the power to our relationship from the very beginning, and he abused it in some ways. The times where I did not do the things he wanted, it made him upset, and I was suddenly in a position of needing to work or beg to get back into his good graces, which wasn't fair or even at all. The playfulness of the dynamic only lasted so long before it actually felt kind of miserable, but it was too late to change it. These are just things to keep in mind should you find yourself in this tricky territory. *Learn from me, kids.*

All in all, though, I feel no type of way about Christian. We knew each other on and off for quite some time, and it's fair to say we "grew up in the Grindr game" together. I had a lot of fun exchanges with him, and he was definitely a comfortable and familiar face (or faceless profile) that I came to cherish over the years. In a lot of ways, our paths to self-discovery aligned. The final time I saw him, we were both in such a better place with our sexuality – both out and not giving a damn, something I doubt either of us would have imagined that first night we spoke. If Christian were ever to read this, I would just want to say "hey – that was fun, thanks for being around…no hard feelings."

[8] CONCLUSION: RESIDUALS

It has been over a decade since Grindr was created, and it has woven itself intricately through the stories of this series. In many ways, it provided an outlet – a way to discover who I was. It immediately connected me to a world of guys that I had no idea how to approach. On countless days, it spared me from my loneliness. Grindr connected me to so many amazing guys going through the same dilemmas as me. It connected me to guys who had been through the same journey – many who gave me advice (good and bad) about what I was feeling. Grindr gave me friendships, experiences, and memories I wouldn't have otherwise known. For those reasons, I am very grateful for Grindr.

By the same token, Grindr connected me with more than my fair share of issues: drama, anxiety, regret, fear, and app addiction, to name a few. Sure, Grindr was just a tool – it's easy to say that I brought these issues on myself. But that's not entirely true. Grindr, by the nature of its design, was created to be addictive for users and profitable for its creators. That specific intent on behalf of Grindr has unleashed a swath of psychological issues that continue to riddle the gay community using it (and long after they stop using it).

You don't fully realize the residual effects of Grindr until you are off of the app for some time. Depending on how long and frequently you used it, Grindr alters the way you think. It completely changes how you approach men, dating, relationships, and sex. For one, Grindr makes you completely jaded. You deal with countless negative experiences and empty conversations during your tenure on the app. Since it is completely geared toward sex, you also lose faith in the idea that a man might have interest in more than just that. Suddenly, you find yourself seeking out men as a sexual commodity – a means to an end. And men treat you the same. It becomes pointless to show your personality, your intellect, or your charm. Over time, you become cold, and that translates into your efforts at serious dating and relationships (whether they are on Grindr or not).

With Grindr, you lose your sense of patience. Everything needs to happen right now, or not at all. If a guy doesn't respond to you immediately and frequently, he is no longer worthy of your attention. If a guy doesn't send you the picture you want, he moves to the bottom of your list. Grindr is built on the idea that you can always have exactly what you want and when you want it. It is always there for you, facilitating the idea that you deserve this. You deserve more and better and you can have it right now. There is always someone around the corner to interact with. There is someone to replace this guy that can't hold a conversation, there is someone to replace a guy who doesn't look how you thought with his shirt off. There is someone to replace your friend with benefits that stopped texting you back, and there is someone to replace your long-term boyfriend, too.

Grindr, with its hyper-focus on stats and images, constantly reinforces the idea of the idealized gay man. The app completely rewards commercial and stereotypical beauty, while downplaying that any other aspect of a man is valuable. All of the attention goes to the muscular, handsome, masculine, and generally white men. You need six pack abs, a full head of hair, a nice beard, a big dick (with photo evidence), and to identify as closely to a traditionally masculine man as possible. That is how you keep the messages flowing.

Sure, we can read that and say "ugh true," recognizing it as a universally valid concept in our community – but think about it a little more. That idealized man is the pervasive and incessant message that Grindr is putting on a pedestal at all times. How many hours, days, months, and years have we spent lingering on an app that glorifies that message? Even if you feel solid with your self-esteem, that environment is completely toxic. The more time you spend in that environment, the more you are affected (whether you consciously feel it or not). The most affected are the most vulnerable members of our community, who deserve better than to be psychologically obliterated by a sex app (but often have no other choice to meet men).

I firmly believe that if you have spent years on Grindr, it will take at least the same amount of time to wean yourself off of the app. It's no different than a drug. For one, most people who delete it will eventually add it back. Out of desperation, loneliness, or sheer boredom – we may *think* we're in control, but the rush of Grindr is very powerful. You go through life without it and recall how exciting it would be to fire it up in various situations – at the gym, on campus, at a concert, in a new city. You recall the rush of a fresh batch of guys messaging you. The rush of an attractive stranger being literally hundreds of feet away from you, engaging in conversation. The alert tones, the notification icons, the thumbnails of flesh-tone images – constantly feeling like you are never alone and always having someone cute to pass the time with.

And that's just the app – what about all of the negative behaviors it leaves you with? It takes just as much time to meaningfully undo those. You have to train yourself to the idea that you should focus on one man at a time. You might have to be more conscious of your personality and attitude, making sure to give the guys you date exposure to your intellect and emotions. You have to put your mental and spiritual needs on par with your physical needs. You have to learn how to become patient, realizing that it may take weeks or months to connect with a guy on the same level as you would within minutes or hours on Grindr. You have to recognize that it takes time to know a man on a level that would enable you to fairly determine compatibility. It's not just a checklist of stats or features – it takes time for a man to open up to you in a way that meaningfully shows his positive and negative attributes – and that's the ride that you have to be present for in a post-Grindr world.

I say this not to leave you discouraged or without hope. There is plenty of hope for those of you interested in leaving Grindr behind, or perhaps you already have but are struggling with its demons. You can actually use your years of experience on Grindr to your benefit. Every time you are tempted to lose focus or relapse, just remember all of the grief that the men of Grindr have caused you. Remember that after those dick pics, the conversation pretty much falls off. Remember how empty it felt to so quickly hook up with a guy but have no other level of connection – wondering if you missed out on something deeper. Remember the times that you thought you were meeting the man of your dreams, only for him to be your personal nightmare. Remember how excited you were for all of those guys who later ignored you. Remember that after years and years of using Grindr, you never quite met a man that treated you the way you wanted and deserved. Despite the fun or satisfying times, try to remember that Grindr most often leaves us feeling empty. Going back to it and restarting this cycle of behaviors can be dangerous.

Not to say that Grindr is evil and no one should be using it. Depending on where you are in your life and what you need – Grindr is a perfectly fine way to build connections and get what you need out of it. A few of you may have even met a boyfriend or husband out of it – consider yourselves lucky! For many of us, Grindr is simply a reality – it is hard to meet gay men without it. At the same time, our options in the app world have exploded. There are plenty of gay men on less sex-obsessed dating apps that are more interested in developing meaningful connections. I think many of us have and should graduate to those types of apps if we are ready for serious connections. A lot of men use both Grindr and those apps, which can be tricky, because it is hard to give the more serious guys the attention they deserve if you are still using Grindr to meet your immediate needs.

Ultimately, Grindr is what you make of it. It can be positive and negative, and most of us have examples of each. If you are going to use it, it is important to remain aware that it is designed to reinforce toxic and negative behaviors, despite the well-meaning intentions of many users and some of the folks at Grindr corporate trying to make things better. With time, I have realized how deeply the app has impacted me. I can't say I regret it – because I don't know where my gay journey would be without it. At the same time, I pay the consequence of this unprecedented tool by having to work on myself even harder to unlearn shallow behaviors and promote the types of relationships I actually want to have. I now know those things will likely never come from an app like Grindr. Unfortunately, nothing good comes easy in life…Grindr has a way of distracting you from that harsh reality for as long as it possibly can.

ABOUT THE AUTHOR

Lex, Esq. is an attorney and blogger born and raised in Southern California. He began his blog The Problem Gays as a passion project to freely discuss LGBTQ+ topics and better connect with his community. *The Grid* series is Lex's first foray into a long-form exploration of the issues he discusses online.

Upon the publication of this book, Lex looks forward to never using Grindr again.

If this book was any level of entertaining or enlightening to you, please take a minute to leave a review on Amazon and/or Goodreads. I would seriously appreciate it.

-Lex, Esq.

Made in the USA
San Bernardino, CA
28 December 2019

62407684R00095